Woman of War

Pam Jenkins

ISBN-978-1-4507-3770-8

Cover designed by: Matthew Clark

To order additional copies of this resource: Contact:

Jabbok Ministries
P.O. Box 1063
Forsyth, GA 31029
478-992-5444
www.jabbokministries.com

Dedication

To the precious Journey Class Ladies at Rock Springs Church, I dedicate, "Woman of War". What valiant women you are, holding the line, standing for truth, loving Jesus and loving one another. You are a light shining in the darkness of this world and I adore each and every one of you. You are brave, fearless and beautiful! I could not have written this study without you. You have this teacher's heart.

Preface

"When I am asked how many demons there are, I answer with the words that the demon himself spoke through a demonic: 'We are so many that, if we were visible, we would darken the sun." (Resource – An Exorcist Tells His Story by Father Gabrielle Amorth, Roman Catholic Priest, Chief Exorcist of the Vatican, Rome, Italy.) There is a spiritual war raging behind the curtains of history, a battle in the unseen world motivating the events in the visible world. The earth and those who dwell upon it are under heavy spiritual attack that has left our world in utter devastation depleting the morals, ethics, health, sanity, conviction, peace and joy from the souls of mankind. This war is not against those enemies clothed with flesh and blood nor is it against any human agency, but against an enemy just as real as any that has ever marched across a battle field or wielded a weapon of destruction. The apostle Paul tells us this in Ephesians 6:12 when he says that our struggle is not against flesh and blood but against spiritual forces of wickedness in the heavenly places. What does this mean for us? We battle that which we cannot see and the saying holds true; "out of sight, out of mind". Though this spiritual war has been waging since the beginning of time, our awareness of it has not. We must open our eyes to the truth that this battle is real and it does exist.

 Like it or not, we are engaged in a life and death battle that rages even now and will continue so until the end of time as we know it. Evil is the present force that operates in the realm of the invisible wreaking havoc in the arena of the visible. We are the target of an all-out assault from a crafty, seductive, very powerful and devastatingly real spiritual force that is described by the Lord Himself as *"the prince or ruler of this world".* As with any other prince, he has a kingdom of loyal followers that live to do his bidding. They are too numerous to count and they are bent on every evil device and torment. They have their being and their purpose in their prince; Lucifer, the evil one, the father of lies, the deceiver, Satan Himself. He is the prince of darkness and his kingdom works tirelessly to drag every soul into the eternal torment of hell. The hour is now and the enemy is warring a great fight against God's creation and in the heavenly places. Even as you read through the preface of this book many have been taken captive by the wicked forces that have, pervaded our world having hurled their chains of bondage upon countless souls.

Satan is real and his realm is ever widening. Into his kingdom of darkness came a woman killed in a horrific accident. This woman had rejected Christ time and time again. Her tormented soul, full of hatred for God and His judgment upon her, cried out from the fiery pit regarding the prince of darkness and his host of demons; *"He is a real spiritual being that has built a kingdom dedicated to the utter destruction of God's Kingdom. He tries to ruin all of you, he and his satellites, the spirits fallen with him at the beginning of time. There are millions of them. They roam around the earth, as thick as a swarm of flies, and you do not even notice it. It is not reserved to us damned to tempt you; but to the fallen spirits. In truth, every time they drag down here to hell a human soul, their own torture is increased. But what does one not do for hatred"* (*Extract from the voice of Fatima, "Cry of a lost soul and the lessons it teaches*). The devil and his forces are haters of God and anything, or anyone, that belongs to God or has a heart for God.

His goal is destruction and his target is you, God's creation. He operates on an unseen plain that we cannot even begin to fathom, and with such power and force affecting every area of our lives: emotional, physical and spiritual. He has the power to embody, to call out the storms from the storehouses of God, to inflict pain and suffering, to tempt, to accuse, to deceive, mislead and even to kill and destroy. Make no mistake, our enemy is stronger than our flesh and we are no match to stand against him, unarmed and without the Lord.

But what is a woman to do? There was such controversy when women stepped up and began demanding for the rights to not only join the military but to be allowed the privilege to enter into combat. Whether or not a woman should have been given this right is not the question that needs answering in our generation, but rather what will the women of God do with the war that has been declared against them in the spiritual realm? We are all at war, female and male alike. Gone are the days of the stories of pitchforks and red tails. And the time to raise arms and station ourselves in battle array is now. We are in a very real and powerfully fierce battle that increasingly intensifies as the day of Christ draws near. From the gates of the throne room of God the battle cry is being raised and it beckons to every child of God to take their stand upon the walls of their city and claim it for God!

What must you and I do, beloved? Where are we to turn? How are we to fight, to stand, to remain steadfast against the raging war wielded against us? How are we to be victorious when facing such a fierce opponent? What about our children, our homes, our families, ministries, health, finances, etc.? Do we fight or simply run to prayer? Do we engage the enemy or do we wait in silence and raise the white flag of surrender? What does God want us to do in the midst of the battle? What is my role in war? These questions are so vitally important to answer and answer them we will. Women are in a spiritual battle the same as men are and unfortunately we are not given a choice as to whether we will go to war or not; we are already in a war and we must not sit quietly in the night! Journey with me, dear one, into the battlefield of the Lord and there, with Word in hand, train for war.

TABLE OF CONTENTS

Pre-Journey Assignment

Welcome to the study of Woman of War! You will begin your study with a pre-journey assignment to help reveal and challenge your thinking. This assignment should be completed before you begin week one of your study. Read through the questions and answer each one honestly and as thoroughly as you can. Take your time with this as it is the ground work for the study that lies ahead of you. It is meant not to frustrate you or spark debate, but rather to open up your heart to receive God's Truth as you delve deeply into the richness of His Word. Often times an awakening of our thought patterns that have been in dormancy for so long, opens a venue for fresh revelation from the Lord. So, bear with me and know that I applaud you, my sweet friend, and I have waged war for you on my knees long before the Lord placed this book into your hands. May God richly bless you as you train for war in His battlefield.

Do you believe there is an unseen world of spirits, good and evil? Why or why not?

Yes, I have been attacked so many times

Do you believe there is a spiritual battle waging war against your life, your soul, your family? Explain your answer, your thinking.

Yes. I am in a constant battle. My family is broken.

Do you believe in Satan and if so, what kind of power do you believe he has? What realm of influence?

He has power over the darkness (very powerful but God is stronger. He deceives, lies, : destroyes, Does all these things to bring you down so he can get power over you.

Do you believe there has ever been a time in your life when you were under some sort of spiritual attack? Give a brief description.

yes, My family is under attack right now and has been for almost 3 years

How do you fight the battles of life; the attacks of the devil?

Through prayer, faith in God knowing He is much more powerful than the devil. Spending time in His word.

How can someone combat depression or any other emotional bondage? What advice would you give them?

Live your life in a way that is pleasing to my savior. Let my light shine in the darkness

Can a person be demon possessed? If so, can they ever be delivered? How?

Yes. Yes. By obeying God - live for eternity do not believe his lies.

What is your role as a Christian in Spiritual Warfare, if any?

To help others have eternal life. Witness to others

Why do you think people get sick? What about those who are mentally ill? Is there any hope for those who are mentally ill, is medicine the answer?

A lot of times I will get sick in the midst of attacks. I think it is the devil. I believe there is hope. Medicine is not the answer

To every woman, who takes this book, who sets her heart steadfastly to study the Holy Word of God, hear Him whisper to your soul; "Rise up, you women who are at ease, And hear my voice; Give ear to my word, You complacent daughters. The battle rages and the forces of evil have come upon us in order to steal, kill and destroy. But it matters not what our enemy will do nor how he turns the heart of men against us; With him is only an arm of flesh, but with us is the LORD our God to help us and to fight our battles…to him who is able to keep you from stumbling, and to make you stand in the presence of His glory blameless with great joy…" May it be said of you, oh valiant warrior of God that you have fought the good fight of faith.

(Isaiah 32:9, II Chronicles 32:8, Jude 1:24)

LESSON ONE

Identifying the Spiritual Battlefield

Identifying the Spiritual Battlefield

Day One

Eugene Peterson wrote…"*There is a spiritual war in progress, an all-out moral battle. There is evil and cruelty, unhappiness and illness. There is superstition and ignorance, brutality and pain. God is in continuous and energetic battle against all of it. God is for life and against death. God is for love and against hate. God is for hope and against despair. God is for heaven and against hell. There is no neutral ground in the universe. Every square foot of space is contested (1997, 122-23).* " The existence of the spiritual realm is very real and powerful,l and can have an effect on the lives of people by touching their health, their families, their emotions, their world and even their future. The Church of Christ and His followers need to exhibit the power of a transformed life by standing firm against the bands of evil. Whether they encounter evil through demonic oppression or activity, either universal or in their personal arenas, the supremacy of the Lord Jesus Christ is a visible force. Fear and ridicule from the world's view of "religious fanatics" have caused many Christians to cower in complacency and trepidation regarding the forces of the spirit world and the acknowledgment of its existence.

The Bible is clear that there is a cosmic battle of good and evil taking place between God and Satan, against the Kingdom of Light and the Kingdom of Darkness. This invisible war is a passionate one that began before you and I were born. Many scoff at the notion of the existence of a spirit world. Whether recognized or not, we cannot allow ignorance, world philosophies, fleshly speculations, Mysticism, reputations, fear, apathy, apostasy, myths or false teachings to govern our beliefs and distort the truth of God's Word concerning the realness of the spiritual realm and the war that is ever raging there. Never before has there been such a curiosity in the phenomenon of the spirit world including such interests as witchcraft, ghostly encounters and demonic possession. This intensity of interest is further proof for those who are anxiously awaiting Christ's return that He draweth nigh. The battle is real and we, as God's children, must learn not only where the battle is fought, but also how it is fought.

There is so much that lies before us in the weeks to come. I want to encourage you to be steadfast and purposeful in your study time each and every week. With the Lord's help, beloved, we will delve into the depths of truth; we will walk out upon the battlefield that has been ordained by God. There, with sword in hand, armed with the weapons of righteousness, we will train for war and declare victory over every spiritual foe and force of wickedness. We will begin our study the same way every day with prayer asking God to teach us truths from His Word and the understanding necessary to apply them to our lives. So, will you take time right now, precious student, and seek the Lord in prayer for His help and His wisdom? Then we will begin our study time together.

The first vital truth a Christian must learn concerning victorious living is learning to identify the enemy and the arenas within which he operates. You cannot fight an enemy that you do not know exists. To see what God teaches us about this enemy we're going to study a passage from Ephesians chapter 6 which is typed out for you and located in the back of your study under the **"TEXT"** portion. Read through the passage from Ephesians and record your first impressions in the space provided for you. List what this passage is about and what it might mean to your life. Also, list any questions you found yourself asking. When studying God's Word, it's helpful if you will learn to interrogate the scriptures. What I mean by this is once you've read through a passage of scripture, then go back through that same passage and ask the 5 W's and an H, Who, What, When, Where, Why and How? For example, who is speaking, what is taking place, when and where are the events, if any, taking place? How am I to obey the commands given, etc.? These questions will open up God's Word to allow you to see so much more through ordinary reading. Once you are finished, answer the questions listed.

My First Impressions of Ephesians 6:10-18

- The LORD will give us His strength
- The full armor of God is needed to stand
- Our struggles are Not against each other but against the wickedness
- We must prepare ourselves to be able to stand for Jesus & resist the devil.
- Know the truth, and be righteous
- Have God's peace in the midst of it all
- Have faith in God so we can extinguish the evil one
- Take your salvation which Jesus died for and the word of God
- Be in prayer, persevere, and petition for all the saints

According to this passage, what is our struggle against?

Against the world forces of Satan.

What is our struggle NOT against?

Flesh + blood

The word **"against"** is a key word in understanding the struggle that we are faced with and it is used numerous times in these verses. Using the color of your choice, take a colored pencil and circle every reference to the word **"against."**

Once you are finished make a list of all the things **"against"** us. There are five!

AGAINST

1. _The schemes of the devil_
2. _rulers_
3. _powers_
4. _World forces of darkness_
5. _Spiritual forces of wickedness in the heavenly places_

So we understand clearly what God is saying to us, turn to your Word Windows Section located in the back of your study and locate the meaning for the word *"Struggle."* Once you've located it, record your findings in the space provided.

Struggle

Wrestling, a contest between two in which each endeavors to throw the other, and which is decided when the victor is able to hold his opponent down with his hand upon his Neck. It is a term transferred to the struggle that Christians have with the power of evil

God identifies for His children that we are in a struggle. This struggle is against the schemes of the devil, against the rulers, against the powers, against the world forces of darkness, and against the spiritual forces of wickedness in the heavenly places. These are the identities of the resistances that we will face in spiritual Warfare and, more importantly, the resistances that have declared war against us. These five resistances or forces, if I may, though unseen, are very real and very powerful. Think about this with me, beloved, when you think of a world ruler, what comes to mind? In other words, what would a world ruler do?

Rule over all his people, Have them do what he tells them to do

When you think about powers that exist, what does this mean to you and how does it make you feel?

Means that I will Need to follow their rules, Not good

What comes to mind when you think about world forces of darkness?

Satan

Or, when you hear the term *"spiritual forces of wickedness,"* how does this make you feel? According to our passage of study, where are these spiritual forces located?

Not uplifting at all. In the heavenly places

The words, "forces, power, and ruler" paint a picture for us of energy, authority, and might; an energy that moves, thwarts, and pushes. It gives the understanding that power is needed if one is to remain unmoved by these forces. Though our eyes cannot see these enemies, they exist and they are bent on destruction. They are the unseen foes exercising their freedom to hurt, distort, control, thwart, frustrate, engage, tempt, demoralize, depress, and try every one of God's creations. It is the five unseen resistances that need to be recognized before we can walk victoriously in every situation of life. These, precious one, are the five principle conflicts waging war against every child of God.

To help solidify these five enemies, I want us to list them on the hand chart in the order they were given to us. Beginning with the thumb, for the schemes of the devil, list these at the top of each finger.

Hand of war

This is a simple question, beloved, but were people on this list?

yes

Were any of your enemies on this list? Were any of the people you are in a battle with now on this list?

Yes, yes

Were circumstances on this list?

Yes

To help us understand what the word **"Against"** means, turn to your Word Windows Section that is located in the back of your study and locate this word and record its meaning in the space provided.

Against

To the advantage of, to be at, Near or by something. Denotes a direction towards a thing or position and state looking towards a thing. Speaks of the goal or limit towards which a movement is directed.

In the light of this word meaning, what does it mean to struggle *"against"* the schemes of the devil, the rulers, powers, world forces and spiritual forces of wickedness?

The devil wants to take advantage

What kinds of battles are we in, beloved? Is it serious? Describe this war in your words based on everything you have seen thus far in our study.

God makes it clear that we are in a war, but not the kind of war of which we normally think. Our war is a Spiritual one, and because it is a spiritual battle, it is engaged and waged in the unseen world. We are laying out the foundational stones of truth regarding Spiritual Warfare. It is not what we can see that we must recognize, but rather that which cannot be seen with the natural eye. This brings us to our Principle for today. Let it sink deeply into the understanding of your heart.

*P*RINCIPLE

SPIRITUAL WARFARE IS ENGAGING THE UNSEEN

In the theatrical world there is an amazing screen that is used for special affects called a Scrim. The versatility of the scrim is invaluable for any director. It gives the director such varied options that it is a must for any successful production. What makes this theatrical tool in such demand is its ability to hide and reveal things by the placement of lighting. When the light is placed behind the scrim, all that is behind it is revealed as though you were seeing it through a kind of iridescent veil. To have a scene hidden until you are ready to reveal it in a particular scene is an added benefit. When you place the light on the front of the scrim, it keeps hidden what's behind it and acts as a backdrop for any scene a director may need. Our spiritual battle is much like a scrim. Our lives are lived in front of the scrim. Behind the scrim warfare is taking place. I believe if God would illumine the scrim from behind we would see a host of evil so vast that our hearts would melt like wax at the sight of it. This is why our Heavenly Father does not allow us to view the enemy with the natural eye. There are exceptions when God on certain occasions, under supernatural circumstances, has unveiled His children's eyes. We will see examples of these exceptions in our study.

First, we must know and understand that our lives are on the front side of the scrim, but our battle lies behind it. As we study God's Word, He will bring to light for us what has been behind the scrim of our life all along. Spiritual Warfare is engaging that unseen world that lies behind our scrim. Today we've learned the first and foremost principle truth to understanding Spiritual Warfare, recognition of the unseen world. Once we've recognized its existence, we will learn how we are engaged in it. War always involves engagement. How do you engage that which cannot be seen? To help you begin to answer this question, let me respond with a couple of questions and information.

Aristotle is credited with identifying the five traditional senses of the human body. Can you list these five senses of the body?

1_____   2_____

3_____   4_____

5_____

Although neurologists disagree to the exact number of senses and what constitutes a sense, Wikipedia lists these five traditional senses:

1. **Sight**
2. **Hearing**
3. **Touch**
4. **Smell**
5. **Taste**

Wikipedia states that humans are believed to have an additional five senses that include pain, balance, joint movement, and time and temperature changes. I believe if we stop and meditate upon these additional senses we will notice that all of these have the potential to affect our five basic senses some of the time..

If the battle is NOT SEEN, what part of our senses will we *not* need to be dependent on?

_____

Are there any of the traditional or additional senses that we've seen which can be affected by the unseen world? Explain why or why not?

_____

_____

_____

_____

_____

I'm sure there are many questions running through your mind at this moment. I just want to encourage you to hang in there with me and stay the course. We are laying the basic foundation of understanding Spiritual Warfare and there is so much more to come, beloved student. This new knowledge and understanding is going to change your life and the way you view things! We have learned that Spiritual Warfare is engaging the unseen, but how does this apply to our life? This brings us to our Life Application for today. Read the Principle with me and then follow through to the Life Application.

Principle: Because Spiritual Warfare is engaging the unseen:

My Life Application Is...

I CANNOT BASE MY ACTIONS ON WHAT I CAN SEE WITH MY NATURAL EYE

Knowing these truths, precious one, what mindset must we strive to develop?

_____

_____

_____

Every week we will put to memory a scripture verse, ammunition for our Spiritual Battle. We will also strive to memorize the entire portion of Ephesians 6: 10-18. Our goal will be to read it through at least once every day. I want to encourage you to read this portion of scripture every morning and every evening as well, if you can! If you will take this challenge, you will find through repeated readings you will store this to memory inadvertently. Ephesians 6:10-18 will be our battle cry! You've already read through these verses several times just in our study time together today, so you are good until tomorrow on this! A good thing to do is to purchase 3x5 index cards with binder rings. If you will write your memory verse each week on these cards, you can have a way to keep them all together and you can add verses from your future studies. I like to call this our RINGS OF FIRE! With these verses, you will have the fire darts of scripture with you at all times!

Our memory verse for this week is an easy one, Ephesians 4:27. Read over it several times and write it on your memory card ring.

Memory Verse

Ephesians 4:27

"...do not give the devil an opportunity"

There is one thing that never leaves us, beloved, the word of the Living God! His word is living and it is active; it is sharper than any two edged sword allowing it to penetrate even to the marrow of our bones. Scripture memorization is attainable if we set our minds to it. Don't listen to the lie of the enemy telling you that you cannot memorize! Truth is necessary for victorious living and it begins not only with Bible Study, but also with Scripture Memorization. So anchor in and press deep to be a good student!

I want us to close every day with a confession of the truth that the Lord has shown us in our study time.

Today's Confession

Lord, I acknowledge that there is a struggle taking place in an arena that I cannot see with my natural eye, but by faith I recognize its existence. I understand that my sight is veiled to this war, but, nevertheless, it is fully engaged at this moment, raging against my life and my family's life and against the souls of mankind. Though there is a war fully engaged, it is not against flesh and blood; therefore, I will not wage war with others, nor engage in fleshly disputes sent by the enemy to exhaust my energy and divert my attention to the arena of the scene. I lift my right hand of war and confess aloud the five resistances that have come against me, the devil with his schemes, the rulers, the powers, the world forces of darkness and the spiritual forces of wickedness in the heavenly places.

Well, my precious warrior, you have finished your first day of study! It wasn't too bad, was it? LOL! I love and appreciate you. And for all the truths to come I cheer you on and encourage you to make a commitment to finish. Our adversary, who we will be learning about in depth, is going to fight you all the way. You must be steadfast and prayed up. Be determined to pray through every obstacle that our enemy is going to hurl in your path while you study God's Word. He wants to hold us captive in the bonds of ignorance. I pray you will not allow him to discourage you. Let these basic truths settle in your heart and mind.

Much love and appreciation and I will see you on day two!

Day Two

The whole world belongs to God and as we've begun our journey of understanding, we know that there is an unseen realm where the forces of good and evil are at war with one another. Whether this truth is embraced, acknowledged or denied by those dwelling upon the earth, it will in no way invalidate it or validate it! The inerrant Word of God is the only standard for truth given to us by Him. While there are volumes of books and countless opinions regarding Spiritual Warfare, there must be but one source for truth and that is the Holy Word of God, the Bible. I've purposely not picked up other studies that expound upon Spiritual Warfare because I don't want a tainted mind. I want to encourage you as well, beloved, to cleanse your mind from any books you may have read on our topic other than the Bible. Because of the varying degrees of teachings that I know are out there, we must seek truth from the Spirit of Truth Himself, the Holy Spirit. We will then be kept on track with accuracy and the ability to rightly divide God's Word.

On Day One of our study, we began reading and studying the passage found in Ephesians 6:10-18. These verses bring to our attention the realness of a Spiritual battle that is taking place behind what we termed as the "scrim" of life. This spiritual scrim cloaks our eye's view of the war that is raging in the supernatural realm that God desires for us to acknowledge. We must have a Biblical view and clear understanding of Spiritual Warfare and the arena within which the battlefield is fought. Many of God's children are living in defeat simply because they have not identified the battlefield. A soldier cannot go to war if he never makes it to the field of battle. Let's take time to pray before we begin our study asking God to open the mind of our understanding and to give us ears to hear and a heart to obey truth. We must always take time to pray, dear student, because truth is not something that is learned, but rather it is something that is revealed to us by God, Himself. We'll begin once you have finished your prayer time.

Let's begin by reading through our passage of scripture that we began studying on Day One, Ephesians 6:10-18. Once you've read through it, let's go back through these same verses, but this time I want you to revisit all the *"Against"* that you circled in Day One. As a way of review, hold out your left hand and name these five unseen resistances aloud as you unfold each finger beginning with the thumb. I want you to use your left hand, beloved, for a reason that we will see later in our study. Once you've spoken these five unseen resistances out loud, write them down in the space provided for you.

1 _____

2 _____

3 _____

4 _____

5 _____

We've identified the five resistances given to us in Ephesians 6:10-18. Let's look at each one of these up close and personal so we can clearly identify them in the day of battle. The first one given to us, the thumb, is Satan's Schemes. In your own words, write out a description of what you think a scheme is or what would constitute a scheme.

A Scheme is:

_____

_____

_____

If Satan has schemes, then what would this make him? A what?

A _____

If you answered "Schemer" or something equivalent, then you answered correctly! Turn to your Word Windows Section and look up the word meaning for *"Schemes."* We need to make sure we understand what a true scheme is. Record your findings in the space provided..

Schemes

_____

_____

_____

Turn to II Corinthians 2:11 in your Bible and note what you learn about Satan's schemes.

_____

_____

_____

Just like the apostles, we are not to be ignorant of Satan's schemes. We must have a spiritual view of the battle by having a spiritual understanding of the enemy and the resistances he uses strategically in the war. Based on your word study, what would Satan have to do to carry out a scheme of his? Think about the meaning of the word and what it might entail.

_____

_____

_____

What would Satan have to be doing in your life to carry out or plot a scheme?

_____

_____

_____

Turn to I Peter 5:8 and note what you learn about Satan and how it relates to scheming.

_____

_____

_____

What is Satan referred to in this verse?

_____

What type of lion is he? What is he doing and why?

_____

_____

Satan's schemes are meant to destroy, because his motives are to devour. We have an enemy that is fierce and meticulous in his planning. Satan has no random acts, but rather they are skillfully devised schemes to ensure a victory. We'll be studying our enemy in greater detail in the coming weeks and we will continue to add to our understanding of the resistances that we battle within the spiritual arena. For now it is vital that we acknowledge that Satan is a schemer and he plans his assaults carefully as he lies in wait to ambush the child of God. Understanding resistance number one is vital to Spiritual Warfare:

Resistance Number One:

SATAN IS A SCHEMER WITH INTENTIONS TO DEVOUR

According to I Peter 5:8, Satan prowls about that he might find someone to devour. Turn to your Word Windows Section and locate the meaning for the words *"Prowls"* and *"Devour."* Write down your findings in the space provided.

Prowls

_____

_____

Devour

_____

_____

In light of your word studies, how would you describe Satan and his schemes?

_____

_____

Turn to Luke 22:31 and note what Satan wanted to do with Peter.

_____

Is Satan a real enemy, beloved? Can he and does he try to invade our lives? If so, explain how and why?

_____

_____

_____

We've identified resistance number one: Satan's schemes. Now let's look at resistance number two as given in Ephesians 6:10-18. Hold out your hand and say these five unseen resistances out loud and note which your index finger is. This should be resistance number two.

Resistance Number Two:

SATAN HAS PUT INTO POWER SPIRITUAL COMMANDERS OVER HIS DOMAIN OF DARKNESS

There is a hierarchy within Satan's Kingdom. With Satan being the King, underneath him are his ordained princes who operate within the domain he has given to them. We'll learn more about these domains in the weeks to come. Right now we only want to establish the order that exists in the unseen world, the world behind the spiritual scrim we've talked about. Turn to your Word Windows Section and locate the meaning of this word *"Rulers"* as used in Ephesians 6:12. This is a long meaning, but it's rich with truth for us if we are going to lay hold of the victorious life that Christ has given to us. So, bear with me, dear student!

Rulers

_____

_____

Turn to Daniel 10:8-21. Read through these verses thoroughly with a heart to understand. Daniel has been given a vision of future events that will take place upon the earth with his people. The truth and realness of the vision given to him by God is so heavy that he is left as a dead man waiting for God to help him understand. An angel of God comes to him and these verses reveal their conversation to us.

Note what hindered the angel from coming and what was happening in the world.

_____

_____

_____

_____

There are rulers or princes as they are referred to in Daniel that have been set in place by their king, Satan. These are not physical princes because we are told they were fighting against the Prince of all angels, Michael, himself. This exposes the unseen world for us, beloved, by allowing us to know that these spiritual leaders are waging war upon the rulers of God. We are laying a vital foundation for understanding Spiritual Warfare.

This word meaning sheds light for us of the internal workings and authorities that Satan has in place. Based on the picture that this word meaning paints for us, I believe that Satan has strategically appointed his four rulers to war over the four corners of the earth. They are his "firsts," his commanders. Underneath their headships fall the spiritual powers that have been assigned under their regimes, and that war in their corners of the world. This brings us to our third unseen resistance.

Third Unseen Resistance:

EACH RULER HAS APPOINTED SPIRITUAL POWERS THAT SERVE UNDERNEATH THEM

Under the princes of darkness there are commanders of the armed forces of Satan. Turn to your Word Windows Section and locate the word meaning for *"Powers"* and record your findings. This, too, is a long word meaning, but it will yield some wonderful benefits in the weeks to come.

Powers

_____

_____

_____

_____

_____

I know that is almost inconceivable for us to think that there exists such an army in the spirit realm. But know this, precious warrior, there is an army of darkness, but there is also an army of light! The battle that wages war is not over strength, but of God's right to reign over all. Satan is no match for God's power so this war is not about strength or might because God is obviously the greatest over all because He is Creator over all! This war is about *reign*, about God's Sovereign right to have control over all and to bring glory to His name. For a time that has been appointed by God, Satan has been allowed to roam, to try and devour, but Satan is still under the authority of God! This brings us to our Principle of truth today.

*P*RINCIPLE

SPIRITUAL WARFARE IS NOT ABOUT POWER, BUT ABOUT OWNERSHIP

What I don't want to happen is for me to paint such a dismal picture of war that I leave you with a feeling of defeat or a shroud of fear. To help us, turn to the following verses and note what you learn from each. In some of these verses Satan is referred to as the "prince of this world." The word "prince" that is used refers to the one that is the Commander- in- Chief, the General.

John 12:31

_____

_____

John 14:30

_____

_____

John 10:29

_____

_____

I John 4:4

_____

_____

We know that Spiritual Warfare is not about power, but about ownership. Then what does that mean to us? Our life application for the truth that we have learned today is absolutely, foundationally necessary for the battle. Read the Principle with me and then follow through to the Life Application!

Principle: Because Spiritual Warfare is not about power, but about ownership:

MY LIFE APPLICATION IS...

There is no power that can overtake what belongs to Him

Praise the Lord! Because God is owner, He will have His way in the end. All of His creation will bow to Him in that final day! Power struggles do not change ownership...not ever! I want us to make our confession of truth that we have learned from our study today. Confessions are made out loud, precious warrior, so read it aloud for all rulers and powers to hear!

My Confession of Truth

Father God, I confess that You are Creator over all, good and evil. You are all powerful and there is no force upon the earth that can overtake You; therefore, there is none that can overtake me. I belong to You and I am in Your mighty hands of protection. I acknowledge that my enemy, Satan, is real and he roams about the entire earth, including my life, and seeks opportunities to devour my life thoroughly. He is a schemer and I am not ignorant to his schemes. I know that there are unseen forces warring with him to bring God's reign to an end. But Father, I confess that Your Kingdom is an enduring Kingdom and One that will never be overtaken no matter how dark it becomes. You are greater than all and I worship You and You alone.

That's all for today, beloved student. Review your memory verse if you need to and I will see you on Day Three. God bless you for all of your hard work today! I'm so very proud of you.

Day Three

Napoleon Bonaparte was one of the most brilliant individuals in history. He was a masterful soldier, an unequalled grand tactician and a most ruthless opponent if you stood as a force against him. Driven, not by wealth, but by power and the thrill of conquest, his understanding of his life can be summed up in his own words; *"A soldier I am, and because it is a special gift, I was endowed with at birth... I have a sense that time is fleeting and I have not a moment to lose."* Though Bonaparte confessed that he believed there was no real force in the world as love that he could determine, but the realness of war was undeniable. How interesting that the most powerful force on earth, love, was a force that one of the most powerful men on earth would never know? Although he missed the truth regarding love, he was right about war; it is very real and it is undeniable. We are born as soldiers, beloved, a gift endowed to us by the Living God when we were birthed into His family. It's not an obligation but a privilege afforded to us by the Greatest Commander of all, the Lord, Himself!

We, too, must acknowledge the forces that have come against God's Kingdom. Napoleon could acknowledge the reality of war because it was his way of life. He engaged in war with full force and brute strength, sparing nothing, and no one, who stood in the way of victory. Spiritual Warfare must become a way of life for us as well and we must make our stand with Heaven in full force, willing to give up all for the sake of victory. We must be unsparing of ourselves and all our possessions, precious one, if we are ever going to have the conquest God has ordained for us. It's the casualties... the losses that usually cause us to run from the battlefields drawn out by God's hand. Where will you and I make our stand? To what will we pour our lives out for and to what will we spill our blood to acquire? Napoleon was so staunch in his beliefs that when he was ordered to eat his food on his knees as punishment when he was in military school he refused declaring, "I bow to no one but God!" If we would have the same militant stance in Spiritual Warfare, oh the ground that could be claimed for the Lord!

Many battles have been lost because of a failure to recognize the force of the enemy. Part of Spiritual Warfare is opening the eye of our understanding to the forces of darkness that have come against the Kingdom of God. In our study time together today we will look at these forces that wage war against God's children. Take time to pray, asking the Lord to speak to your heart and give you the wisdom that you need and an obedient heart to apply the truths He reveals to you. Then we'll begin.

Let's begin by reading through our passage of scripture we've been examining this week, Ephesians 6:10-18. I want us to take our left hand, and beginning with our thumb, name the five resistances of Spiritual Warfare. If you need to look back at our previous days of study or at Ephesians, then feel free to do so. Once you've spoken these five resistances out loud, take a minute and write them down in the space provided.. This will help you seal them into your memory for good!

The Five Unseen Resistances of Spiritual Warfare

1._____

2._____

3._____

4._____

5._____

Take a colored pencil and underline every reference to the word(s) "force or forces" in these verses. Use the color of your choice. Once you've finished, write down which forces we struggle with according to Ephesians 6:10-18. Note what type of forces they are and any thoughts you have regarding how they might affect the world or your own life on the chart provided. Once you've finished your list, answer the questions listed.

The Forces Against Us

Where are these forces found?

_____

_____

Where is their sphere of influence?

_____

_____

Are these forces found in the light?

_____

Turn to your Word Windows Section in the back of your study and locate the meaning for the word *"Forces"* as used in Ephesians 6. Record your findings in the space provided.

Forces

_____

_____

These forces that are given to us in Ephesians can refer to the devil and or his demons. Let's remember how they have just been described for us so we can understand the realm in which they operate and how they operate. They are described as "world forces of darkness" and "Spiritual forces of wickedness.". Based on their description, in what kind of activity would Satan and his demons be engaged?

_____

_____

What are we told is their sphere of influence, their arena of power?

_____

_____

Turn to Daniel 11:31-37 in your Bible. As you read this passage referring to the Antichrist who is to come in the end times, note what will arise from him and what they will do.

_____

_____

In the end times, beloved, there will be such occurrences happening in the world as never before. One such occurrence is the rising of an Antichrist who will come and bring peace to Israel. A seven year covenant with Israel will allow them to rebuild their beloved temple and will restore to them the right to offer sacrifices unto God. However, half way through this seven year peace treaty the antichrist will break the agreement. The prophet Daniel tells us that from the antichrist, who is Satan incarnate, forces will arise to desecrate the temple which they have built. Satan, the antichrist, will walk into the temple and set himself up for worship as a god. These forces that will arise from him are "world forces of darkness and spiritual forces of darkness" that his demons have been commanded to carry out his plans.

What I want us to see is this: Satan's plan has always been to take God's place of reign, to overthrow His Kingdom in order to set up his own. This is what his forces are working toward this very hour. This brings us to our principle for today.

*P*RINCIPLE

FORCES ARE WAGING WAR TO OVERTHROW GOD'S THRONE

This is why, precious student, that the war is not about power, but about God's right to reign and rule over what belongs to Him. This is why the attack is aimed at the very throne of God. If they can overthrow God's throne, they can set up their king in His place, the Prince of Darkness. I want to show you this in scripture. Turn to Ezekiel 28:12-18. As you read through this passage, know that the King of Tyre is making reference to Satan. Write down what you learned about Satan in the space provided.

Satan
King of Tyre

_____

_____

_____

_____

_____

What did God find in Satan's heart? What did He do as a result?

_____

_____

_____

_____

Satan has set his heart from the beginning to take the place of God. Satan wants to take control over every area where God reigns, and the places that God is seeking to reign, Satan seeks to thwart. Can you name any areas where God is currently not reigning where He desires to reign ? These could be areas in your own life; areas of your country, your job, your church, your finances, etc. Give this some thought and write down what God brings to your mind.

_____

_____

_____

_____

How can our awareness of these areas and Satan's plan to rule help us in Spiritual warfare? Think about how Satan puts up his resistances. Through what? How should this knowledge affect the way we think, act, and live?

_____

_____

_____

_____

Knowing the forces and their purpose to overthrow and to overtake is a powerful truth for Spiritual warfare. It is the very foundation needed to grow in our knowledge of the battle. If there are any areas that you have surrendered to God's authority, you can know that Satan will scheme to overthrow God's reign there. If there are any areas in your life where God is not currently reigning, you can rest assured that Satan will raise up his forces to thwart any surrender in your life that would allow God to have control there. This should put us on our guard to know that God's right to reign is always under attack. Read through our principle of truth and then follow it through to our Life Application.

Principle: Because forces are waging war to overthrow God's Kingdom

My Life Application Is...

I MUST TAKE MY STAND TO DEFEND WHAT BELONGS TO HIM

Here's the very painful part of this truth, beloved, the choice we make to surrender unto God's reign or not to surrender will be determined by the side we take. Any areas that we have not surrendered unto God's control are areas that Satan has claimed victory over. This is a difficult truth to take hold of, but it is vital to victorious living. What are areas in your life that you have not surrendered? What areas have you surrendered that are being threatened for a hostile takeover by Satan? What measures should you take in order to protect what belongs to God or to yield unto God what is rightfully His? Over what areas has Satan raised the victory banner? I've left you with a lot to meditate upon so I ask you to soak these truths up and take them to the Lord in prayer.. Let's finish our study time together with our confession of truth that we have learned today.

My Confession of Truth

Lord, I confess that You have the right to reign and to rule every area of my life and over all of Your creation. Your kingdom will have no end and there is none who are above You. Your Kingdom will have no end and You will reign victorious. You desire to have every area of my life surrendered unto Your full control and You are deserving of it. I recognize that Satan devises plans and sends his forces of wickedness and darkness to dethrone You and to enthrone himself. I acknowledge that the spiritual battle is for my heart and I confess that my heart belongs to You

.

That's all for today, dear one. Remember what the battle is about and that you are the intended target. Review your memory verse and I'll see you on Day Four.

Day Four

Jesus said in John 9:4; "*We must work the works of Him that sent me, as long as it is day: the night cometh, when no man can work.*" In the past few years, increasing awareness of spirit activity on a territorial level has emerged and is continuing to grow as our world is further engulfed in darkness. Evil deeds that were once carried out only under the cloak of darkness have boldly pronounced their presence even in the light of day. Satan's activity is intensifying and is no longer content to operate within the shadows. There is a boldness of evil as never before. Home invasions are commonplace, smash and grabs are so numerous that law enforcement can't catch up, let alone bring prevention. Murders, human trafficking, child pornography, sex crimes, drugs, abuse and prostitution are rapidly increasing. Never has our world found itself in such a place where immorality, mysticism, the occult, confusion, hatred, violence, fear, insecurity, a sense of hopelessness and anarchy have dominated the hearts and minds of people. What is happening in our world, beloved? The words of our Lord are coming to pass in our generation; *night is coming*. I read a report by Don Rogers and his ministry's encounters with Spiritual Warfare of which he said the following:

"Over the years I have encountered this kind of activity (spiritual warfare) and have been able to learn from it. Understanding the dynamics of the spirit world is not for the curious or those who are fascinated by such things. This kind of understanding brings great responsibility. We become accountable to use what God reveals to us in helping others. There is often a price to be paid. The path is often difficult and only those who know how to persevere in faith are successful."

Spiritual Warfare is intensifying because the hour for finality is drawing nigh! God has given us the blessed right to open up His Word and learn the truth about the warfare we are in. With the knowledge He reveals to us, we become even more accountable and responsible to join the ranks of heaven and fight for God's Kingdom. The Church has remained in complacency for too long and the call from Heaven shouts, "It is time!" We must work while it is day, beloved, because night is coming when none of us will be able to work. We have a short window of opportunity to glorify the Lord and to fight the good fight of faith. He has shown us that the battle is real and we are most certainly in it to the end! With this in mind, let's turn to the Lord in prayer and seek His blessings upon our study time together as we finish out our first week together. Begin when you are finished.

Hold out your left hand, precious warrior, and recite the five unseen resistances of Spiritual Warfare for God's children. See if you can say them without looking. Say these several times aloud. Always begin with your thumb and if you need to peek, go ahead. Once you've declared these out loud a few times, take a minute to write them down as well. Hearing, writing, speaking and seeing make for cement in our memories!

1. _____

2. _____

3. _____

4. _____

5. _____

Let's turn to Ephesians 6:10-18 in our "TEXT" section of our study and read aloud our War cry. Remember, we are trying to read through these verses every morning and every evening through our study of Spiritual Warfare. Before we're finished, you will have committed these powerful verses to memory, tucked away in your heart and mind forever. When you are finished, answer the questions that follow and turn to any scriptures noted and record your insights.

What type of battle are we in?

_____

_____

_____

Who or what is our struggle *not* with?

_____

_____

Is this struggle just a myth or is it real? Explain your answer.

_____

_____

_____

It's not only important to acknowledge that a spiritual struggle is present and is very active, but it's absolutely imperative that we recognize what a spiritual struggle is and what a fleshly struggle is. To help us a little bit turn to the following scriptures, note the struggle, who was involved and why.

Philippians 4:3

_____

_____

Colossians 2:1

_____

_____

Beloved, what are your greatest struggles? Who or what do you battle in your Christian walk?

_____

_____

What do you exert the most spiritual effort over? List these out and also how you expend your energy, time, resources..

_____

_____

Do these battles, these struggles in your life, fall into the category of flesh and blood or could you safely mark them under the spiritual side under one of your five resistances? Explain why or why not?

_____

_____

Are there any forces in your life, any struggles that you feel are from flesh and blood, either internally or from other people that you recognize, but just don't know how or what to do to change it? If so, write these out so you can see them in print.

_____

_____

_____

Satan's greatest scheme is to entice us to war with those things that find their origin in the flesh. By doing so, we have no energy, no mind and no desire to engage in the spiritual battle taking place. In doing so, Satan has just removed you as a threat to his kingdom because you are not a weapon of God's. His scheme has been the same from the beginning, to divert our attention away from the battle so he can gain ground that belongs to God. That brings us to our

*P*RINCIPLE

OUR FLESH HAS NOT BEEN CALLED INTO BATTLE

We do not arm ourselves with the flesh when we are going into a Spiritual battle. Spiritual battles must be fought in the spirit because the flesh has no power in the war between good and evil. Where defeat is present, the flesh has gone to war. Powerful truth to embrace for us, beloved, powerful truth!

Turn to the following verses and write out all you learned from each. Note where and how victory is obtained or how the spiritual battles are fought.

II Corinthians 10:1-4

_____

_____

Romans 8:36-39

_____

_____

Psalm 18:34-50

_____

_____

Based on the verses we just read, how can these truths help you in understanding Spiritual Warfare?

_____

_____

When we find ourselves in a confrontation, we must remember our first foundational truth of Spiritual Warfare: there is an unseen battle taking place in the spirit realm and, therefore, our struggle is not against flesh and blood. Second, because it is a spiritual battle, we cannot send in our flesh to fight it. This was our life giving Principle today and, as you read it through once more follow it with our Life Application:

Principle: Because our flesh has not been called into battle

LIFE APPLICATION

THE SPIRIT MUST GIRD ITSELF FOR WAR

Much of our difficulty comes when we try to equip our flesh to war in a spiritual battle. We arm ourselves with the weapons of words that hurt, defeat, tear down, destroy, or through retaliatory deeds aimed at those we deem as our enemies. Sometimes we build ourselves a fortress and we retreat in fear, or hide behind the wall of denial we've erected to pretend it's not there at all. We send out our own resistances that are "seen" rather than recognizing the unseen resistances that have come against us. The first act we must take in Spiritual Warfare is accepting the responsibility to arm our spirit for war rather than our flesh. What are you arming, beloved, your spirit or your flesh? What are you sending into battle? As we come to the close of our week's study, I want you to go back through our week together and fill in the chart that reflects the Principles and Life Applications we've learned for each day of study.

OUR WEEK IN REVIEW

Day One

Principle:
Life Application:

Day Two

Principle:
Life Application:

Day Three

Principle:
Life Application:

Day Four

Principle:
Life Application:

Let's close out our week with our confession of truth. Read it aloud to the Lord and claim the truth by faith!

Confession of Truth

I confess my utter weakness and vulnerability to utter failure when I decide to send my flesh into battle. I am not able to war against the powerful forces that have set themselves to destroy me. I am absolutely weak and doomed to defeat apart from You, O Lord. I confess my need for You and my dependency upon You. Arm my spirit with the truth of Your Word, O Lord. Thank You for hearing this warrior's cry for help. Train my hands for war and lead me to victory.

Thank you for working so hard this week. Take a few moments to answer the Personal Evaluation Questions to help bring the truth of what God has revealed to us all the way home to the heart. I'll leave you with these praises to you for being such a wonderfully diligent warrior this week! Hang in there, precious friend, we've only begun to lay a foundation. There is so much to build up in our storehouse of truth.

Personal Evaluation

Do you take Spiritual Warfare seriously? How does it affect your everyday decisions, words and actions?

_____

_____

_____

_____

_____

How do you defend yourself against the Devil's schemes, against the forces, rulers and powers that have declared war upon your life?

_____

_____

_____

_____

_____

_____

_____

Are you at war with others?

_____

_____

_____

_____

What are the resistances in your life? How are you coping with these?

_____

_____

_____

_____

Has Satan claimed victory over the areas that God once reigned over? Are there areas that you have not surrendered under God's authority?

_____

_____

_____

_____

What are your weaknesses that might leave you vulnerable to the schemes of the devil?

_____

_____

_____

_____

Session Notes

_____

_____

_____

_____

_____

_____

_____

_____

_____

_____

_____

_____

_____

_____

_____

_____

_____

_____

_____

_____

_____

_____

LESSON TWO

Knowing Your Adversary

Knowing Your Adversary

Day One

During the Vietnam War thousands of soldiers lost their lives in a war that would prove to be one of the worst times in all American history as well as the country of Vietnam itself. The Vietnam War cost the United States 58,000 lives and 350,000 casualties. It also resulted in between one and two million Vietnamese deaths. It was the longest war in American history and the most unpopular American war of the twentieth century. Even today, many Americans still ask whether the American effort in Vietnam was a sin, a blunder, a necessary war, or a noble cause, or an idealistic, if failed, effort to protect the South Vietnamese from totalitarian government (*Digital History)*. The greatest factor of difficulty for this war was fighting an enemy that was unseen. It was like trying to fight an invisible force because of their endless hidden tunnels and their cunningness in war. How can you fight an enemy you cannot see? It's akin to trying to box the air and win.

Spiritual Warfare has an enemy in much the same way except God not only warns us of His unseen presence, but He reveals how to stand firm in the midst of the battle. Listen to the Apostle Peter's words referring to our enemy, *"Be of sober spirit, be on the alert. Your adversary, the devil, prowls about like a roaring lion, seeking someone to devour. But resist him, firm in your faith, knowing that the same experiences of suffering are being accomplished by your brethren who are in the world. After you have suffered for a little while, the God of all grace, who called you to His eternal glory in Christ, will Himself perfect, confirm, strengthen and establish you."(I Peter 5:8-10).* Our adversary Satan, also known as the devil, is mentioned numerous times throughout the Word of God. Although there are many popular myths and beliefs about this evil being, it's clearly evident that he is an adversary to God's children. While many have concluded that he is not a real being but rather a personification of the wickedness that abides in the world, God's Word reveals that he is a personal entity and an evil being who affects the human race by his actions.

The greatest strategy for war is knowing your enemy. Spiritual Warfare demands an awareness and *knee knowledge* of our adversary because he has declared war upon our lives and the lives of those we love. How well you know your enemy will determine the level of protection and stability you have in the face of war. A child of God should have no alarm, no fear of the enemy, and they should not lack knowledge of his tactics. This week in our study, we will look at what God's Word teaches us about the enemy so we will not be ignorant children. Ignorance is the place where Satan wants to keep us! Seek the Lord before you begin your study time and I'll meet you back here when you are ready.

Let's hold up our left hand and speak aloud our five resistances. Say this several times to help engrave them so deeply that they leave an indelible mark upon your mind! As we learned last week, these five resistances are very real and extremely powerful. At the head of these forces of evil and darkness is the devil, our adversary. Although we are not sure exactly when the angelic hosts (the spirit world) were created, evidence suggests to us that they were present at Creation and possibly made during the first few days of creation. Look up the following two passages of scripture and note what you learn about the angelic world, also referred to as the Host of Heaven, The Morning Stars or Sons of God.

Jeremiah 9:6

_____

_____

Job 38:4-7

_____

_____

_____

The passage from Job suggests that the angels were present when God "laid the foundations of the earth.". This could refer to when God separated the dry land from the water on the third day of creation. Though we don't know exactly when they were created, we can examine what God reveals about the creation of Satan. Before we do that, I want you to take a few minutes to write down what you believe to be true about Satan. Draw from what you've heard in your life, studied, been taught, assumed, etc.

My Belief About Satan

To help us know what God says about him, we're going to look intently at two passages of scripture that will help furnish a picture for us of Satan's original condition and the reasons for his loss of that position. Both passages are addressing an earthly king, but at the same time they are giving us the long-term implications of an exalted angelic being by the name of Satan. Both passages are typed out for you.

Read through each one separately and, as you do, draw a black "S" over every reference to Satan which in these passages will be the King that is being referenced. Be sure to mark every pronoun as well. When you have finished marking the text, make a list of everything you learned about Satan, on the chart provided.. Be sure and ask your interrogating questions (who, what, when, where, why and how). This will yield greater insight if you'll take the time to ask these questions out loud. So, I encourage you, wonderful student that I know you are,… don't rush your assignment.!

Ezekiel 28:11-19

11. Again the word of the LORD came to me saying, 12. "Son of man, take up a lamentation over the king of Tyre, and say to him, Thus says the Lord GOD, "You had the seal of perfection, Full of wisdom and perfect in beauty." 13. "You were in Eden, the garden of God; Every precious stone was your covering: The ruby, the topaz, and the diamond; The beryl, the onyx, and the jasper; The lapis lazuli, the turquoise, and the emerald; And the gold, the workmanship of your settings and sockets, Was in you. On the day that you were created, They were prepared. "14. "You were the anointed cherub who covers, And I placed you there. You were on the holy mountain of God; You walked in the midst of the stones of fire." 15. "You were blameless in your ways From the day you were created, Until unrighteousness was found in you." 16. "By the abundance of your trade You were internally filled with violence, And you sinned; Therefore I have cast you as profane From the mountain of God. And I have destroyed you, O covering cherub, From the midst of the stones of fire."

17. "Your heart was lifted up because of your beauty; You corrupted your wisdom by reason of your splendor. I cast you to the ground; I put you before kings, That they may see you."

18. "By the multitude of your iniquities, In the unrighteousness of your trade, You profaned your sanctuaries. Therefore I have brought fire from the midst of you; It has consumed you, And I have turned you to ashes on the earth In the eyes of all who see you. 19. "All who know you among the peoples Are appalled at you; You have become terrified, And you will cease to be forever."

Satan, According to Ezekiel

_____

_____

_____

_____

_____

_____

Where does God tell us Satan was?

_____

_____

What is he referred to as, "the guardian" of what?

_____

Write a brief description of his character according to this passage?

_____

_____

Describe his outward appearance?

_____

_____

What was found in his heart?

_____

_____

What did God do to Satan as a result of this?

_____

_____

Now let's read through and mark our next passage of scripture; Isaiah 14:12-15. Mark every reference to Satan and make your list the same way you did with Ezekiel. Answer the questions that follow.

Isaiah 14:12-15

12. "How you have fallen from heaven, O star of the morning, son of the dawn! You have been cut down to the earth, You who have weakened the nations." 13. "But you said in your heart, 'I will ascend to heaven; I will raise my throne above the stars of God, And I will sit on the mount of assembly In the recesses of the north.' 14. 'I will ascend above the heights of the clouds; I will make myself like the Most High.' 15. "Nevertheless you will be thrust down to Sheol, To the recesses of the pit."

According to the prophet Isaiah, what did Satan plan to do?

_____

_____

Whose place did Satan want to take?

_____

_____

Based on what we've learned thus far, who created Satan?

_____

_____

God hates a prideful heart and I believe it's because of the death that the spirit of pride can bring. He has experienced firsthand in His own home, Heaven. One of God's greatest and most powerful creations became ambitious and proud and made the bold step to try and dethrone the One Who created Him in order to take His place. Look up the following verses and note what you learn about Satan from each.

I Timothy 3:6

_____

_____

Revelation 12:3-4 (Satan is referred to as the "Red Dragon" and the "starry hosts" are angels.) Note how many angels followed Satan when he left Heaven.

_____

_____

I John 3:8

_____

_____

John 8:44

_____

_____

Based on what we've read thus far, what has Satan been trying to do from the very beginning?

_____

_____

It's imperative, as God's beloved and Satan's enemy, we know the truth about Satan's origin. Find the *"My Adversary"* chart located in the back of your study and write out what you've learned about the origin of Satan in the appropriate column marked "His Origin." Fill in any other truths that you have learned regarding our enemy in the column that is relative. You will want to note when he was created, who created him, what was he like, etc. We'll continue filling in this chart as we continue our study of our adversary.

How do you feel this information can help you in Spiritual Warfare?

_____

_____

_____

_____

Relative truth is what we want to glean, beloved, because it will enable us on the battlefield. Because we have an unseen enemy, we must learn his motives, his plans, his methods and how to predict him so we can make ourselves ready. Defeat is inevitable with an unknown enemy. This brings us to our Principle for today.

*P*RINCIPLE

OUR ENEMY IS UNSEEN BUT NOT UNKNOWN

Jesus said in John 8:32; *"You shall know the truth, and the truth shall make you free"*. It is not the existence of truth that sets one free but, rather, it is the knowing of truth that releases the captive. God doesn't want His children to be blindsided or live in fear because of the unknown. He is a God Who desires for His children to be prepared and that means having knowledge of those things that we need to know concerning our enemy. We cannot fight an unseen enemy that is unknown. Knowledge is power, beloved student, when it is applied to life. God gives knowledge and understanding to us in order to empower us. Turn to the following passages of scripture in your Bible and take note of how knowledge of truth benefits our lives.

John 12:35

_____

_____

II Timothy 1:12

_____

_____

Hebrews 3:10

_____

_____

Knowledge is the first step in our defensive stance, beloved. Knowledge removes the veil of ignorance and affords us a secure position in the battlefield of the enemy. Read through your principle and follow it with our Life Application for today.

Principle: Because our enemy is unseen but not unknown then…

My Life Application Is...

KNOWLEDGE WILL BRING RECOGNITION

How do we recognize those things that cannot be seen, those things that are not visible to the physical eye, yet, we know that they exist? For example, love is not a visible entity, but it can be heard, felt, experienced and expressed. It can bring pain and devastation and even temporary pleasures. We can see love by the evidence of its existence. When we learn truth about our adversary, we will learn to recognize the evidence of his existence. His presence or activity in our lives or the lives of those we know and love will be easily discerned. Knowledge brings recognition and recognition brings defense! Without this knowledge, this truth of who he is, we are left defenseless. Our memory verse this week is actually two verses. These verses are going to help as we add them to our warfare verses for use in battle. Read over your memory verses for this week several times to help you begin to memorize it.

MEMORY VERSE

I John 3:7-8

"Little children, let no one deceive you; the one who practices righteousness is righteous, just as He is righteous; the one who practices sin is of the devil; for the devil has sinned from the beginning. The Son of God appeared for this purpose, that He might destroy the works of the devil."

Let's read over our confession of truth as we call it a day. I know I've worked you hard today and I am so proud and very honored that you would join me, shoulder to shoulder, to study the Living Word of God. What a blessed right we have been given from Heaven to open up God's Word and glean the richness found therein. I'll see you on Day Two!

My Confession of Truth

Father God, I confess that I have an unseen enemy who has declared war on You and all that is rightfully Yours. I must accept the responsibility to learn what Your Word teaches me about him so I will not be unaware. No one can learn these truths for me, it is my choice to make and make it I do. I will not be ignorant to my adversary or to his ways. He is corrupt in his heart and his goal is to overthrow Your throne by destroying all that belongs to You, O Lord. I belong to You; therefore, he is my enemy too. You are my protection, Father God, and in You I am kept safe from the adversary.

Day Two

Paul wrote to the church at Thessalonica, *"For we wanted to come to you - I, Paul, more than once - but Satan hindered us."* Some years ago while waiting in a Tokyo subway station with a small group of other believers, we had an encounter that none of us would ever forget. We had been sent on assignment by a Mission Organization to go to an "unreached people group" in a small string of islands which was part of the country of Japan. We had faced such opposition on this entire trip and one battle after another had left our group doubting. We wondered if we should even get on this small plane that was scheduled to take us out to our destination. Fear had crept in and most in our group were at the point of changing their minds, unwilling to take the flight. We did the only thing any good Baptist group could do; we took a vote! I'm still not sure where God's will actually fit into that plan, but at the time we were desperate, fearful, and a long way from the safety of our homeland. After the vote our group was divided, and yes, we even managed to have a church split on the mission field!

At the lowest ebb of our indecisiveness, up came a man to the little circle of the "let's go" group. He was aged, clothes tattered and dirty. His teeth were darkened from lack of dental care and he spoke in the old Japanese dialect that you would hear only in the countryside, which meant he spoke no English. I must admit at first I thought to myself, "Oh no, he wants money"…sad, but true, beloved. I was tired, fearful and disappointed in the way our trip was turning out and at that moment I was not feeling the mercy as I had no money to give him. I asked the Lord to help me be kind and patient to the man who clearly was bent on telling us something. He spoke very emphatically and kept repeating the same thing over and over again. I replied in what little Japanese I could speak and said, *"I'm sorry, but I do not understand Japanese."* Whenever he would finish speaking, I would repeat the same thing over and over again. He acted as though I was not even there, let alone speaking. Finally, after becoming highly irritated, he spoke in English as plain as I've ever heard; *"Get on the plane and go, everything will turn out alright."*

To this day I don't know if the Lord allowed our ears to hear him speaking in English or if He allowed him to speak to us in English. Either way, the Lord gave us understanding to the message He obviously wanted us to hear. I believe *"many have entertained angels unaware."* Whoever or whatever this man was, his message was too supernatural for us to ignore. We chose to listen loud and clear and with fear and trembling, not for the enemy, but for God and His work. We boarded a little plane and fulfilled God's purpose for that time in our lives.

You see, beloved, the Lord had us going on no ordinary trip, for this would turn out to be for the furtherance of the Gospel. We had a mission, but we also had an adversary who was also on a mission. He was trying to thwart the way and hinder us from going. We, as God's children, must not only recognize that we have a very compelling enemy, but we need to know the ways and the impediments which he will try to force upon us in direct opposition of God's plan. The Apostle Paul understood this and he identified it for what it was. We must do the same! Pray before you begin and then we will jump into our day of study together.

I want to encourage you to continue reading through Ephesians, our text for every morning and every evening until you have it memorized. If you will do this daily, you will memorize it! Let's start our study time together with a review of our left hand! Hold up it up and recite the five unseen resistances that Christians face. To help cement it in, write these five resistances out in the space provided..

My Five Unseen Resistances

1. _____

2. _____

3. _____

4. _____

5. _____

I'm so proud of you, precious student! Way to go! Today we're going to be looking at the realm in which Satan has been allowed to operate. We want to identify his tactics, his methods, his goals and his targets. In the "Text" section of your study book which is located in the back, you will find Job chapters 1 & 2. Read through these chapters of Scripture to get an overview of what's happening in these verses. When you are finished, write down your initial thoughts of the events that are taking place. Write the actions of Satan and anything else you find interesting. There is a box provided..

First Impressions of Job Chapters 1 & 2

_____

_____

_____

_____

_____

_____

_____

Now let's read through these two chapters once more, but this time mark every reference to Satan the same you did on Day One of our study and make a list of everything you learned about Satan on the chart provided.. Remember to interrogate this passage after you make your list.

SATAN

What powers did Satan have?

_____

_____

_____

_____

What limitations did Satan have and why?

_____

_____

_____

According to what we've read, to whom does Satan answer? Who defines the boundaries in which he must exercise his power?

_____

_____

Who brought Job to Satan's attention?

_____

_____

Was Satan familiar with who Job was? Explain why or why not.

_____

_____

_____

What question did God first ask Satan? What was Satan's reply?

_____

_____

If I were to ask you, "Why do you think Satan was roaming about upon the earth"? What would you say?

_____

_____

To shed some light for us from God's Word, let's turn to I Peter 5:8 and note what Satan is doing in this passage of scripture.

_____

_____

What is Satan compared to in I Peter 5:8? What do you think this means to us?

_____

_____

In the Bible a person's name would represent their character, their nature and conduct. Although there are several titles given to Satan in the Bible, I want us to look at the two that are most familiar and that we've just seen in Job and I Peter. Turn to your Word Windows Section and locate the word meanings for *"Satan"* and *"Devil"* and record your findings.

Satan

_____

_____

Devil

_____

_____

_____

How did Satan live up to his name in the life of Job?

_____

_____

_____

Let's read through our two chapters of Job once again, but this time I want you to draw a circle around every reference to Job using the color of your choice. Once you have completed your markings, make a list of everything you learned about Job in the box provided.. Note his character, his lifestyle, his heart toward God, his heart toward his children, etc.

Based on Job's life and character, what made him a target of Satan?

_____

_____

_____

What changed in Job's life as a result of Satan's resistances? List these areas out.

_____

_____

_____

_____

Make a list of Job's losses?

_____

_____

_____

_____

Job, the Man

What does this show us about Satan's power? Think about how he affected the life of Job and the areas of attack. What was the first area of attack?

_____

_____

_____

_____

Big question, beloved,…how did Satan's attack against Job affect the lives of others, his family, friends, etc?

_____

_____

_____

Satan was created in beauty and splendor according to God's perfect design. He was the Holy Guardian Cherub who was over the most Holy place of all, the altar of God. He was created as the most powerful angelic being over all the others. There is no doubt that God loved him. He was designed to protect and serve God in the most sacred place, Heaven. But something happened in Satan's heart; he was not content to serve, but rather he wanted to be served. He did not desire to worship His creator, but rather he sought to be worshiped. He became prideful, arrogant, and as a result, his great pride caused him to stumble by turning his heart against God. He gained support for his cause, and built a following of one third of the angelic hosts of heaven. They went with him when he abandoned the position God had given to him.

Satan is a spirit being and cannot be killed as ordinary men; he was created to live forever. Having great power and a vengeance fueled by his wrath towards God, he roams about the earth like a lion hungering for the blood of the saints. Although he operates on the leash, God gives him, he can manipulate the weather, destroy our homes, take the lives of those we love, and inflict our own bodies with physical suffering. Satan stirs the hearts of our enemies so that they come against us; destroying, stealing, and killing all that is precious to us. He shows no mercy and is intent on one thing, utter destruction of all who are dear to God. Since Job was dear to the heart of God, Satan marked Job with suffering. Job was righteous and he feared the Lord, His God. This made him an adversary of the devil and a target of his wrath. Strike the child of God and you strike the heart of God. We must not underestimate our adversary, beloved. This brings us to our Principle today.

$\mathcal{P}$RINCIPLE

THE MARK OF SATAN'S DESTRUCTION IS AIMED AT THOSE WITH WHOM GOD IS PLEASED

The mark of Satan's destruction is aimed towards all of those who love God and have a heart to serve Him. This makes Satan angry! We must understand that he knows about every child of God who is a threat to his kingdom and an asset in God's. God pointed Job out to Satan because He wanted it known that He had a child upon the earth who loved and feared Him. God was declaring to Satan; *"This is one that you didn't get, and he belongs to me!"* This tells us that God delights in the lives of His children so much that He sparks the conversation to His enemy. What honor it brings to God's name when He can declare before all the sons of God, "Have you considered my servant?" Before all the angelic hosts, good and bad, God was bragging on His child, as any loving, doting Father would. You have to love that!

Go back and review your markings of Job in your text and write out all the things in his life that you believe were pleasing to God.

_____

_____

_____

How did Job respond to the suffering that had come upon his life?

_____

_____

What did his wife tell him to do as a result of his suffering? What was Job's response to her?

_____

_____

Had Job sinned before Satan's attack on his life? Did he sin afterwards?

_____

_____

What does this tell you about adversities and losses that come into our lives?

_____

_____

To lose someone we love is so difficult, but to lose all your children and all your belongings in one day is unbearable and unimaginable for most of us. This was most definitely a catastrophic event in Job's life and yet, it was not due to his sin; it was not a form of punishment. It's our nature to ask, *"What did I do to deserve this?"* when tragedies happen, rather than acknowledging the One Whose hands it came from. Let me ask you a question, beloved, "Would your lifestyle be a threat to Satan's Kingdom?" Would God be able to brag on you before the sons of God? Why or why not?

_____

_____

We've seen our Principle for today, but what does this mean to us? Read aloud our Principle and follow it with your Life Application.

Principle: Because Satan's mark of destruction is aimed at those whom God is pleased with, I can know:

LIFE APPLICATION

SATAN'S ADVANCES ARE EVIDENCE OF GOD'S APPLAUSE

Is it any wonder that James told God's people to *"consider it all joy when you encounter various trials?" (James 1:2)* We shouldn't consider the pain of the trial as joy, but rather the reason the trials come. This makes it more bearable to know that it can be God's evidence of His affection but, more importantly, His delight in us. Let me show you a couple of scriptures that ring this truth loudly and clearly. Turn to each and note what you learn.

II Timothy 2:3 (note what kind of soldier is to suffer?)

_____

_____

I Peter 3:14

_____

_____

Acts 5:41

_____

_____

II Thessalonians 1:2-4

_____

_____

Do you see it, beloved warrior? Satan's advances are God's mark of pleasure upon our lives! We have reason to rejoice in the attacks because God has smiled upon us in the day of Satan's visitation and he has to get permission from our Father beforehand. This brings comfort to us because we can rest assured that Satan is not doing anything in our lives of which God is not absolutely and totally aware. He's not only allowed it, but He's determined the boundaries of adversity as well. Take a few minutes and fill in any information regarding Satan on your *"My Adversary"* Chart which we began working on Day One of our study. Praise the Lord for truth! As will be our finish every day, let's read our confession of truth!

My Confession of Truth

I confess O Lord that You are the Most High God and You rule over all, the good and the bad. My adversary, the devil, roams about like a lion seeking out someone to devour. But You, O God, set his boundaries and every act he does in my life. Satan has to get your permission first. I confess that I am not in the hands of my enemy, but I am in the hands of my God! My enemy is Satan because he was Your enemy first. I take my stand with You, God and there I will remain all of my days.

Truth is everything, dear student,…everything. It is your guide and it is your rear guard. Hold tightly to it, even in the darkest of times. It will never falter and it changeth not. I pray that you will rise above the ashes of devastation and proclaim that God delights in you. You are His and He is ever aware of what happens to you. ***Satan's opposition is God's applause!*** Now that's a "slap your neighbor and yourself" truth, right there! Write this power truth in the box provided. We're going to call this our **"POWER BOX."** This is a life- changing and life- living truth for us. Write it big, precious, because this is a BIG TRUTH!

POWER BOX

Let's close out our time together by reviewing our memory verse together and by writing it out in the space provided for you including the scripture reference. This will help you commit it to memory. I'm so proud of you, sweet warrior.

Memory Verse

_____

_____

_____

_____

_____

Day Three

There have been a number of encounters reported with Satan over the ages; from face to face encounters, to voices and possessions. Saint Dunstan, a tenth-century bishop of Canterbury, reported that he was in his workshop making a metal chalice when Satan suddenly appeared in front of him. To defend himself, he seized the intruder's nose with a pair of red-hot tongs. The great Protestant reformer, Martin Luther, reported dozens of encounters with Satan. On one occasion he threw an ink pot at him in sheer reaction to his physical appearance. Based on what we've seen in God's Word thus far, we know that our enemy, Satan, was created by God in beauty and with purpose. He was more beautiful than words can describe and he was elevated above the other angelic hosts. God gave to him great power and the responsibility of guarding the very altar of God. But Satan became proud because of his beauty and magnified himself in his heart even above God, Who created him. He caused a revolt in heaven and because of it, God cast him out and one third of the angelic hosts went with him. After all, Satan is a schemer. He is attractively beautiful and his power can be very enticing.

God created him for good; for the holiness and beauty that is found in fulfilling one's purpose. No doubt that it must have broken the heart of God to have one of His most special Creations turn against Him, in order to overthrow His Kingdom. And then, to have one third of the others turn away from Him as well, and follow another. It was a deep wound of the heart. This wound is still deep today, beloved. Satan is still scheming to turn others away from God; wanting them to follow and serve him with their lives. He continues to stab at the heart of God, through thievery, by taking what is rightfully the Lord's. But you and I are taking steps right now through the study of God's Word to learn the truth about our enemy. We're going to continue our study of our adversary, the devil, in our time together today. If you haven't already done so, take time to pray, asking God to bless your study time and to open up your mind so you can understand the Scriptures and behold the wonderful truth from His Word.

As a quick review, can you lift up your left hand and call out loud the Five Unseen Resistances? See if you can and when you have been successful, meet me back here! We saw on Day Two of our study the power of suffering and loss that Satan can be permitted to have in the life of the righteous. When allowed, he has the power to kill, destroy, inflict physical suffering, use the weather, and entice others to steal, attack the innocent, and perform signs and wonders from the sky. He can even blind the hearts of our friends and spouses. All of this was seen in the life of Job. Satan was attacking Job's faith and trust in God; trying to move his heart to curse God and renounce his faith in Him. Although Job lost everything, he did not sin against God. What a testimony of passing through the fire and coming out pure!

Today, we want to back up in time and look at the first encounter that mankind had with Satan. Typed out for you is Genesis chapter three and is located in the text session at the end of your book. In this passage, Satan is referred to as the serpent. Read through it once to get an overview of the events that are taking place. When you are finished with your initial reading, go back through and mark every reference to the serpent, including any pronouns.

Once you've read through this chapter, go back and read through it once again, but this time mark every reference to the serpent in the same way we've been marking references to Satan. Once you've finished, make a list in the box provided of all that you saw about Satan from marking the text. Remember to ask your questions and meditate upon the Word! Answer the questions given when you are through making your list.

The Serpent

Did Satan know what God had spoken? Did He know the Word of God, the commandment of God? How?

_____

Who did Satan approach first and how did he approach them?

_____

_____

What accusations did Satan give or imply about God's character?

_____

_____

What did Satan want Eve to do? Explain why?

_____

_____

What would happen to Adam and Eve if they ate of the Tree of the Knowledge of Good and Evil?

_____

_____

Let's go back through Genesis chapter three and this time mark every reference to God by drawing a purple triangle over each. The triangle symbol represents the Holy Trinity and purple is for Royalty. Once you've marked every reference including any and all pronouns, make a list that shows all that you learned about God from this chapter in the space provided below. Make sure that you take your time with this chapter, beloved student, because the events in this chapter cost God His only Son. It was an act on God's part that would spill His own flesh and blood upon the soil of the earth that He might redeem His children from the grasp of our enemy. Read this hall of redemption with a reverent heart, ears ready to listen, and eyes seeking to look upon the heart of a merciful God.

What kind of relationship did God have with Adam and Eve?

_____

_____

How did God establish to Adam and Eve that He was the One they should obey? How do you think they knew that He was God?

_____

_____

What did Adam and Eve do once they disobeyed God by eating from the Tree of the Knowledge of Good and Evil?

_____

_____

How did this affect their relationship with God? What emotions did they experience when they heard Him calling for them? What was their response to God?

_____

_____

_____

God

Adam and Eve hid themselves from God because fear had gripped their heart. This is not the first time sin had entered into the world as we know it, but with it came *fear* for the first time. There was no fear upon the earth until sin came. Sin and fear are synonymous with one another, beloved, and a fear of standing before God. They were not afraid until they heard the voice of God calling them. Some day we will all hear the voice of the Lord call us to come to Him and it is in that day that fear will grip the hearts of all those who are found in sin. How will you be found, precious warrior? Satan desires above all else to keep us enslaved in fear, so that we will not glorify and honor God with the right relationship. He knows that sin is the channel through which fear will enter. This is food for thought for us.

Did Satan leave or did he hang around? Explain your answer and review the scriptures to find your answer. Why do you think he did or didn't stay around?

_____

_____

_____

How is Satan described in Genesis Chapter Three?

_____

Satan was described as "more crafty" than all the other creatures. Turn to your Word Windows Section and locate the meaning for the word *"Crafty"* and record your insights in the space provided for you.

Crafty

_____

_____

_____

According to our Five Unseen Resistances, Satan's Schemes rank right at the top of the list; our thumb! In the light of your Word Study for crafty, how does this relate to what we see Satan doing in the garden to Eve? Was he scheming and, if so, what do you think was his scheme?

_____

_____

_____

Who was Satan really after? Was it Adam or Eve or someone else?

_____

_____

Take a few minutes and read through the first two chapters of Genesis, so you can understand what took place before Satan's scheme was put into place. Once you have finished, write out in your own words what God's order was. For example, who was to rule over the earth, etc? Who was man to obey? Were they warned about an enemy? What was God's warning to them, if any?

_____

_____

_____

Satan went after God's authority, didn't he? Remember that he is power hungry, prideful and a schemer. He intends to break down God's Kingdom by weakening God's authority upon the earth. This is what he did in the Garden and this is what he continues to do today in the gardens of our lives. He told Eve something that is very striking to think about. He told her," that God knows in the day that you eat of it you will become like Him…" Isn't this what Satan was after? Isn't Satan the one who wanted to be like God and take His throne over? Yet, he turned the truth of what he wanted and made God out to be a liar. Satan uses his own desires and plans to make them seem as though they are God's plans. Listen carefully to this truth, precious one.

*P*RINCIPLE

SATAN COUNTERFEITS HIS PLANS TO LOOK LIKE GOD'S

Do you see how subtly he threw his plans in under the disguise of God's plan? All that Satan gives will always be a counterfeit of what God's is. And the realization is that just like Adam and Eve, most Christians never even realize it's happening. We will learn through this study how to combat this and guard ourselves against the schemes of the devil. Like the Apostle Paul said and may we join him in saying, *"We are not ignorant of his schemes."* Even now, through your study of the Word, you are removing ignorance of the devil's schemes because you are learning truth. But how do we recognize Satan's counterfeits? Follow me and let's dig a little deeper in Genesis.

Why did God create man and woman? What was His pattern for making them? What does this tell us about the life they were created to live?

_____

_____

God created man and woman in His image. Look up the meaning for this word *"Image"* in your

Word Windows Section located in the back of your study book and write down what you find in the appropriate space provided..

Image

_____

_____

_____

Look up the following verses and note what you learn from each regarding our image and the image of the Lord.

Romans 8: 29

_____

_____

I Corinthians 15:49

_____

_____

II Corinthians 3:18

_____

_____

Colossians3:9-10

_____

_____

We live in a day where people are very image conscious. The truth is that God created us to be image conscious, but with His image, not ours! Herein lies the danger, the line that we must be careful not to cross.. God's image is our concern and displaying Who He is to the world, so that all can know Him and He can obtain all the glory. When God's image is not seen then it is not known. If He is not known, then, neither will a counterfeit be known when it comes along. We must guard His image in our lives at all cost. God, Who knows all in His wisdom, made us in His likeness in order to protect us, so we would have the truth and realness of Him within our own selves. This way it can never be lost, beloved. We shouldn't have to search for God past our own noses. Read our Principle out loud and then follow it with our Life Application.

Principle: Because Satan counterfeits his plans to look like God's.....

LIFE APPLICATION

WE MUST GUARD GOD'S IMAGE

We are first and foremost God's image bearer. When sin entered into the world, His image was marred because sin mars holiness. This is Satan's strategy in dethroning God by attacking His image. I pray that we will be women who recognize that the devil's plans will always be to distort the image of God, by perverting Who He is. What better way to do this than to attack His image bearers! Let's close out our time together by reviewing our memory verse for the week by reading over it several times to help it stick. The older I get, the more glue I need girls! When you're finished gluing, let's read out loud our Confession of Truth for today.

My Confession of Truth

I am a creation of God's own hands. I am His design, His masterpiece and I was created for His glory. God fashioned me after Himself and therefore, I am to display His image. I am an image bearer of the Living God Who reigns in the Heavens. I am to reflect His image because God desires to be seen and known by all of mankind. Satan is my enemy because he is the enemy of God. He desires to lead me astray so the image of God will be distorted. He will use trickery, doubt, confusion and lies to mislead me. I am not to listen to the voice of the enemy, but I am to remember what God has said and hold fast to it. God never lies, but Satan is the father of all lies; therefore, he will never tell me the truth. When I am presented with a plan, a thought, a desire, I will hold it next to the image of God and see if it reflects Who He is. I will turn away from all that is not of God and that does not reflect His holiness.

64

I am so proud of you, mighty warrior that you are! Hold fast to the truth and guard the image of God in all that you say and do, and in every decision you make and counsel you receive in the light of Who God is. I pray that you will continue reading aloud our War cry from Ephesians chapter 6. Read it every morning and every night as many times as you can. Don't forget the enemy's tactics and the goal that he has set in his heart to mar the image of God and thereby, dethrone God and Who He is. We were not created to tarnish!

Much love for you ,
Pam

Day Four

We've reached the end of our second week together, beloved student, and I am thanking God for you as I sit and write these words. God has so much in store for us if we will keep pressing on to the finish line of our study. Remember, we have an enemy who will use every tactic and scheme to keep God's image hidden, to distort it and to tarnish Who God is in the eyes of the world. Our enemy is fierce and very real, even if he is unseen. The evidence of his power and destruction are visible all around us, and often times, even in the ruins of our own lives, we see his finger prints. We cannot sacrifice our future for past losses and we were not created to be defeated. You and I bear in our bodies the handprints of God who fashioned us in our mother's womb that we might be an exact reflection of Who He is. He sent Jesus so we would see and understand what we are to be like in order to be like the Father. When God's image was marred, God stepped in and corrected the plot of the devil by declaring payment of His only Son, Jesus. God's image cost Him His only Son and therefore, it is a priceless gift from Him.

Today, we will continue looking at the different ways that Satan attacks the image of God. We want to begin with our prayer time, seeking God's anointing upon our study time and asking Him to allow us to know truth and therefore, know Him. Let's start our study time by holding up our left hand and declaring our *Five Unseen Resistances* aloud! You go, girlfriend! Now that you've made your declaration of truth, let's dive in to the richness of God's Word. Ready? Read through the passage of scripture from Luke Chapter 4 that is typed out for you and is located at the end of this week's lesson. As you read, note what is happening in the space provided. Record the events and the people involved and any other important information that you see.

My First Impressions

_____

What do we see Satan doing in this passage?

_____

_____

Based on the questions he asked Jesus, whose place is Satan trying to take? What was he trying to do?

_____

_____

Let's read through these verses in Luke once again, but this time we want to mark every reference to Jesus by drawing a red cross over each including any and all pronouns. When you are finished marking the text, go back and review each cross and note what you learn about Jesus from each. For example, where was He? What was He doing? Why was He doing it? What was Jesus' state of mind and what was His life like at the time? How did He handle the enemy, etc? You are asking all of your questions so you can glean wonderful truths from the Word of God. When you have finished, make a list of truths about Jesus based on these verses.

Jesus
_____
_____
_____
_____
_____
_____

What was Jesus' spiritual life like at the time He went into the wilderness?

_____

_____

What was happening to Him for the forty days He was in the wilderness?

_____

Describe Jesus' physical state when Satan began to question Him?

_____

_____

What did Satan tempt Jesus with? What was his scheme?

_____

_____

How did Jesus withstand his schemes; his temptations in His weakened state?

_____

_____

Go back through these verses and mark every reference to Satan in the same way that we have been marking him. Note anything new you learned about Satan that you have not seen before or that you did not know.

Satan Insights

_____

_____

_____

_____

Jesus was full of the Holy Spirit; following the leading of the Spirit by going out into the desert. It was at this place that Satan came against Him. What should this tell us about Satan and how he operates and what kind of people he targets?

_____

_____

_____

How does this compare with what we learned about Job? What similarities do you see?

_____

_____

_____

_____

_____

What differences were there?

_____

_____

Job loved and valued his family. He prayed for them daily and sought God's favor for their lives consistently. Satan targeted his weakness; the place where he could inflict the most pain. Jesus was at a weakened state; the Scriptures tell us that He was hungry and rightfully so, because He had been fasting for forty days. Satan targets our weak areas and if we do not have one, he will wait until we are in a weakened state to attack, like he did with Jesus. Satan's goal is always to attack a weak spot, create a weak spot, or wait until you are in a weak spot to attack. I want us to write these three truths out in the box provided for you.

Satan's Schemes

_____ **a weak spot**

_____**a weak spot**

_____ **until you are** _____ **a weak spot**

Remember, beloved warrior, we are not to be ignorant to Satan's schemes. This brings us to our Principle of truth for today.

$\mathcal{P}$RINCIPLE

SATAN USES OUR WEAKNESSES TO GAIN ENTRY INTO OUR LIVES

Our weaknesses or weakened conditions are potential doors for Satan to enter through. It is those doors where we must learn to set up guards or to lock all together. We will, precious student, we will. We are continuing to lay a foundation and we will build upon it each and every week. We've already increased our knowledge and awareness of Satan's tactics and how he operates. I want us to see more of this truth that is found in God's Word. Look up the following verses and note what you learn about Satan from each. Take note of what weakness or weak spot was present or created.

I Chronicles 21:1-7 (David was in fear of retaliation from the people of Gath because they had just killed one of their giants.)

_____

_____

I Corinthians 7:1-6

_____

_____

_____

Luke 22:31 (Peter had just said he would die for Jesus)

_____

_____

II Corinthians 11:13-15

_____

_____

I Corinthians 2:9-11

_____

_____

Acts 5:3

_____

_____

II Corinthians 12:7

_____

_____

Isaiah 14:12

_____

_____

Satan weakens the nations because he knows that it will in turn weaken the people. Satan attacks on many different levels; from our personal lives, to our jobs, our cities, our counties, and even our nation. His strategy is always the same, to weaken or attack in a weakened state. Satan takes advantage of weaknesses to elevate himself. We must remember this trait, precious one, we are never more like the enemy than when we take advantage of another's weakness or the state of weakness they may be in. Let's read through our Principle for today and follow it with our Life Application.

Principle: Satan Uses Our Weaknesses To Gain Entry Into Our Lives

LIFE APPLICATION

WE PROTECT OUR DOORS

Our doors are our weaknesses and recognizing them as doors is a step toward victory. We must take preventive measures at all times. Learning to barricade our doors by allowing God to strengthen our weak areas is difficult, but knowing that when we are weak, He is strong and greater is He who is in us than he who is in the world gives us reason to be solid. Take a few minutes to fill any new information about Satan on your "**My Adversary**" chart. Let's read our confession of truth for today.

My Confession of Truth

Satan is a liar, a deceiver and a schemer. I will not succumb to his power or influence. I know that God is stronger than any weakness or any weakened state where I may find myself. I will trust Him with all the entryways that Satan may try and penetrate. I will not be ignorant any longer and I will stand watch so I may identify my enemy.

Let's look back at this week's Principles and Life Applications as way of review including today's by filling in the Week in Review.

OUR WEEK IN REVIEW

Day One

Principle:
Life Application:

Day Two

Principle:
Life Application:

Day Three

Principle:
Life Application:

Day Four

Principle:
Life Application:

We will close out our week together with our Personal Application time. This is always a truth session for us. I want you to know that I love and appreciate you so much. Answer the following questions that will help search our hearts with the truth we've learned this week.

Personal Evaluation

Can you recognize when Satan is attacking?

_____

_____

_____

_____

Can you identify your weak areas?

_____

_____

_____

_____

How do you think Satan has attacked your life thus far?

_____

_____

_____

_____

_____

How does your life reflect the image of God?

_____

_____

_____

_____

_____

Are you a target of Satan? Why or why not?

_____

_____

_____

_____

_____

Luke 4:1-15

4 Jesus, full of the Holy Spirit, returned from the Jordan and was led around by the Spirit in the wilderness

2 for forty days, being tempted by the devil. And He ate nothing during those days, and when they had ended, He became hungry.

3 And the devil said to Him, "If You are the Son of God, tell this stone to become bread."

4 And Jesus answered him, "It is written, 'MAN SHALL NOT LIVE ON BREAD ALONE.'"

5 And he led Him up and showed Him all the kingdoms of [b]the world in a moment of time.

6 And the devil said to Him, "I will give You all this domain and [c]its glory; for it has been handed over to me, and I give it to whomever I wish.

7 Therefore if You [d]worship before me, it shall all be Yours."

8 Jesus answered him, "It is written, 'YOU SHALL WORSHIP THE LORD YOUR GOD AND SERVE HIM ONLY.'"

9 And he led Him to Jerusalem and had Him stand on the pinnacle of the temple, and said to Him, "If You are the Son of God, throw Yourself down from here;

10 for it is written,

'HE WILL COMMAND HIS ANGELS CONCERNING YOU TO GUARD YOU,'

11 and,

'ON *their* HANDS THEY WILL BEAR YOU UP,
SO THAT YOU WILL NOT STRIKE YOUR FOOT AGAINST A STONE.'"

12 And Jesus answered and said to him, "It is said, 'YOU SHALL NOT PUT THE LORD YOUR GOD TO THE TEST.'"

13 When the devil had finished every temptation, he left Him until an opportune time.

Jesus' Public Ministry

14 And Jesus returned to Galilee in the power of the Spirit, and news about Him spread through all the surrounding district. **15** And He *began* teaching in their synagogues and was praised by all.

My Adversary

His Origin	His Appearance	His Strategy	His Intent	His Methods	His Ending

Session Notes

LESSON THREE

Exposing the Darkness

Exposing The Darkness

Day One

The idea of angelic beings, demons and evil spirits can seem somewhat farfetched to some people and full fledged crazy to others. Then, there are those who simply are on the fence line with the idea, and don't know what to believe. Whether one believes in it or not, there is the undeniable interest and drawing to understand the existence of, or explore the possibility of existence of the unseen world. Hollywood has proven this to us time and time again with the large audience following of hits such as; *Touched by an Angel*, *Highway to Heaven*, *Promise Land*, *Charmed*, *Angels and Demons*, *Harry Potter*, *Ghost Whisperer*, *Medium*, *Paranormal Activity* and *Sixth Sense* to name a few. There is an undeniable attraction to the supernatural, be it good or bad. With this interest comes an unseen vulnerability that often leads us naively into arenas that God does not want us to enter. With the knowledge God has given to His people, there are boundaries that He has put in place to protect us from wandering into spiritually dangerous places. We must respect the boundaries God has given to us, while embracing the truth of the unseen world made available to us.

Let me give you some truths (facts) about the spirit realm that we can glean from God's Word and that you will verify as you continue through this study. The Bible acknowledges the existence of angels. Out of the sixty-six books of the Bible, thirty-four of them make reference to the angels. Jesus taught us about angels in numerous verses such as Matthew chapters 8, 24, and 26, etc. We are taught that God created them as spirits, yet, personal beings having intellect, emotions, and a will. An angel can only be in one place at one time and although they are spirit beings, they can appear in the form of men, in dreams, natural sight with human functions, seen by some and not others. Angels do not die because they are spirit beings created by God for an eternal existence. They have communicable attributes greater than man, but less than God. They are much more powerful than humans, but not more powerful than God. They are organized and ranked such as: One Archangel, Chief Princess, Seraphim and Cherubim. They are ministering spirits as God directs and they were created to attend to Him through service, worship and praise. They carry out His government and they are His messengers to people, nations and other spirits.

Satan, as we studied last week, was God's chief angel at one time, created in absolute perfection and power. He sinned in his heart against God and he swept one-third of the angels of heaven away to join his regime. It was like a mutiny in Heaven against the Captain of Heaven Himself, the Lord God Almighty. These angels chose to leave their Creator and follow the created because they were led into sin by the schemer himself and he enticed them with power. These spirits are too numerous for us to count and since they abandoned God's service, their host has been enlarged, as we will see in our study time this week. What was created in beauty and in all that was good and holy, has now crossed over into a very dark realm. The spirit world changed the day that Satan took his army of followers to begin a new kingdom, birthed out of hunger for power and through deceitfulness. Something happened that had never been known before, not even with mankind, WAR. This war, beloved, still continues today and is increasing in power daily. We know this is true because God has revealed these things to us. One doesn't have to look very far into the condition of the world to see that there is a very powerful force of evil spreading throughout the whole earth.

Even with the astounding evidence before us today, there still continues to be a mountain of controversy over the existence of angels, spirits, and demonic oppression and possession; is it real, is it not? Can we trust what has been documented and what we have seen on television, what Hollywood gives to us? Whether what we see on documentaries is true or not is not a responsibility God gave to us, but rather to know His truth, so we will know when error comes along. In our study of spiritual warfare, beloved, we must lay aside all that we have received from the world or have been indoctrinated with, so we can pick up the garments of truth and clothe ourselves with the power of God's Word. We must not be tossed to and fro by the things we see, hear, or read about, that happens in our world. We must be grounded, cemented in, immovable, and totally involved with and in God's Principles, Today we will continue looking at the unseen enemies that every child of God has. Make sure you have prayed to the Lord, asking for His enlightening and protective presence as you study His Word. Many of you are under attack now because you are studying the Word of God! When you are finished, we will begin.

Let's dive into our study of God's Word today by reading through the book of Jude, which is only one chapter, so no worries! It is typed out for you here so you can have it close and it will not take up too much space. As you read through this chapter, take in what is being said and note the time in history. Write down any first impressions of Jude and its warnings to us.. List these thoughts on your "First Impressions Chart."

Jude 1:1-25

[1]Jude, a bond-servant of Jesus Christ, and brother of James, To those who are the called, beloved in God the Father, and kept for Jesus Christ:

[2]May mercy and peace and love be multiplied to you.

[3]Beloved, while I was making every effort to write you about our common salvation, I felt the necessity to write to you appealing that you contend earnestly for the faith which was once for all handed down to the saints.

[4]For certain persons have crept in unnoticed, those who were long beforehand marked out for this condemnation, ungodly persons who turn the grace of our God into licentiousness and deny our only Master and Lord, Jesus Christ.

⁵Now I desire to remind you, though you know all things once for all, that the Lord, after saving a people out of the land of Egypt, subsequently destroyed those who did not believe.

⁶And angels who did not keep their own domain, but abandoned their proper abode, He has kept in eternal bonds under darkness for the judgment of the great day,

⁷Just as Sodom and Gomorrah and the cities around them, since they in the same way as these indulged in gross immorality and went after strange flesh, are exhibited as an example, in undergoing the punishment of eternal fire.

⁸Yet in the same way these men, also by dreaming, defile the flesh, and reject authority, and revile angelic majesties.

⁹But Michael the archangel, when he disputed with the devil and argued about the body of Moses, did not dare pronounce against him a railing judgment, but said, "The Lord rebuke you!"

¹⁰But these men revile the things which they do not understand; and the things which they know by instinct, like unreasoning animals, by these things they are destroyed.

¹¹Woe to them! For they have gone the way of Cain, and for pay they have rushed headlong into the error of Balaam, and perished in the rebellion of Korah.

¹²These are the men who are hidden reefs in your love feasts when they feast with you without fear, caring for themselves; clouds without water, carried along by winds; autumn trees without fruit, doubly dead, uprooted;

¹³wild waves of the sea, casting up their own shame like foam; wandering stars, for whom the black darkness has been reserved forever.

¹⁴It was also about these men that Enoch, in the seventh generation from Adam, prophesied, saying, "Behold, the Lord came with many thousands of His holy ones,

¹⁵⁾to execute judgment upon all, and to convict all the ungodly of all their ungodly deeds which they have done in an ungodly way, and of all the harsh things which ungodly sinners have spoken against Him."

¹⁶These are grumblers, finding fault, following after their own lusts; they speak arrogantly, flattering people for the sake of gaining an advantage.

¹⁷But you, beloved, ought to remember the words that were spoken beforehand by the apostles of our Lord Jesus Christ,

¹⁸that they were saying to you, "In the last time there will be mockers, following after their own ungodly lusts."

¹⁹These are the ones who cause divisions, worldly-minded, devoid of the Spirit.

²⁰But you, beloved, building yourselves up on your most holy faith, praying in the Holy Spirit,

²¹keep yourselves in the love of God, waiting anxiously for the mercy of our Lord Jesus Christ to eternal life.

²²And have mercy on some, who are doubting;

²³save others, snatching them out of the fire; and on some have mercy with fear, hating even the garment polluted by the flesh.

²⁴Now to Him who is able to keep you from stumbling, and to make you stand in the presence of His glory blameless with great joy,

²⁵to the only God our Savior, through Jesus Christ our Lord, be glory, majesty, dominion and authority, before all time and now and forever. Amen.

First Impressions

_____

_____

_____

_____

_____

Let's read through these 25 verses of Jude once more but this time mark every reference to angelic beings by drawing a circle around each using the color of your choice. Be careful not to miss any of the pronouns that refer to them as well. Make a list of all you learned about these angelic beings. Remember to ask questions that will help open up truth to you; Who, What, When, Where, Why and How? Make a list of the truths you learned.

Angelic Beings

What are we told that these angels did?

_____

_____

_____

As a result of their actions, what happened to them?

_____

_____

Who was their leader?

_____

Who are we told prophesied about these angels?

_____

_____

Go through the text and underline every reference to Enoch with the color of your choice and write out what you learned about him from your markings. (Remember the pronouns.)

Enoch

_____
_____
_____
_____

I want us to see the genealogy of the Enoch spoken of in Jude because we are told he was the seventh from Adam. We also want to see what we are told about him and what happened to him. Look up the following passages that refer to Enoch and note what you learned about him and his life from each.

Genesis 5:3-24 (This passage is a little long, but it will take you through the ancestral line of Enoch.) Note from which son of Adam Enoch descended.

_____

_____

_____

Hebrews 11:5

_____

_____

What is the one thing that stands out about this man?

_____

Turn to your Word Windows Section and look up the meaning of Enoch. Record your findings in the space provided for you.

Enoch

_____

Luke 3:37 gives us the genealogy of Jesus' line through his earthly father, Joseph. Jesus comes from the line of Adam's son, Seth. From that line would come Abraham, Isaac, and Jacob. Enoch was a man who walked with God so intimately, that the scriptures tell us one day God took him home bypassing death altogether. We're told in the book of Jude that Enoch was a prophet and prophesied about evil and the coming of the Lord to execute judgment. It is here in the book of Jude that Enoch's prophetic words are given credibility. Some of Enoch's prophecies were discovered with the Dead Sea Scrolls. I want to share a portion of those writings that were found in our study today, but I want to add a disclaimer. I am in no way advocating that the writings of Enoch, which were discovered or to which Jude makes reference, should have been considered as part of the canon of Scripture. I do, however, want to acknowledge a small portion of his writings for their historical value to our topic of study. I believe that its truths have been somewhat validated by being referenced in the book of Jude. So, I think we are on safe, spiritual ground, beloved, because I would never lead you somewhere that was not spiritual. Although Enoch's writings were not added in the Holy Scriptures, I want to show you the verses from Jude that quote Enoch's writings to help give you some assurance. Then, I want to show you the actual portion of writing that he was quoting as found in the prophecies of Enoch. Keep in mind that we can know, the writer of Jude not only knew of Enoch's writings, but he had read them and regarded them as truth, as a reliable source.

Jude 1:14-15
¹⁴It was also about these men that Enoch, in the seventh generation from Adam, prophesied, saying, "Behold, the Lord came with many thousands of His holy ones, ¹⁵⁾to execute judgment upon all, and to convict all the ungodly of all their ungodly deeds which they have done in an ungodly way, and of all the harsh things which ungodly sinners have spoken against Him."

This verse matches with a portion of Enoch's prophecies which states…

"And behold! He cometh with ten thousands of His holy ones, to execute judgment upon all, and to destroy all the ungodly; and to convict all flesh of all the works of their ungodliness which they have ungodly committed, and of all the hard things which ungodly sinners have spoken against him."

Do you see how these line up, beloved? Enoch's writings that were discovered and referenced in Jude also give insight into the Fallen Angels that we'll glean from a little later. II Timothy 3:16-17 tells us that all scripture is inspired by God and is profitable for teaching, for reproof, for corrections, for training in righteousness so that the man (or woman) of God may be adequate, equipped for every good work. The book of Jude is God-inspired and I believe with all my heart, we can trust what it tells us and any author's truth it embraces as well. With that in mind, let's continue our course of study for today.

It's the fallen angels that I want us to look at today. Let's look at what scripture tells us about them. Look up the following verses and note what you learned from each.

Genesis 6:1-5

_____

_____

_____

II Peter 2:4

_____

_____

_____

What did the "sons of God" do that was displeasing to God?

_____

_____

As a result, what resulted from their relationship with women?

_____

_____

What did Peter tell us that these angels did? What wording did he use to describe their acts?

_____

_____

Although we are not told just how many, we are told that these fallen angels, who followed Satan out of Heaven, looked upon the daughters of men in a lustful way. They took them as their wives and went into them and bore children. These children were giants or Nephilim and were very evil. This angered God and in His wrath He decided to flood the earth in order to purge it from all the uncleanness. Remember, we want to know truth about our enemy so we are not "ignorant" to their schemes or their power. Truth removes fear too, precious one, and there is no need to fear our enemy because God reigns over all! Read Jude verse 6 and write out what these angels did and what their punishment was as a result.

_____

_____

God took these fallen angels who had fathered these children and locked them away in a place called the abyss because of what they had done. They will not be released until an appointed time during the tribulation. At which time they will inflict much pain upon the people who are living upon the earth. The children born to them, however, died in body only during the flood; their spirit lived on. It is believed that these spirits are recognized today as demons or evil spirits that are referenced throughout the Bible. Enoch's prophecies also substantiate these further for us with the historical detail of events that he gives us. There has been much speculation and controversy over the differentiation of fallen angels, demons and evil spirits. Although I am certainly no scholar, beloved, and no authority, I do believe that, regardless of the differences between them, there is one common denominator: They are all evil and against God's Kingdom.

A large part of the Church today embraces the writings of Enoch that were discovered, simply because of their historical accuracy with the rest of scripture and because it is referenced as truth in the Word of God. I do want to give you some interesting information that has been gleaned from these writings as they relate to our course of study. As always, beloved, we need to sift everything through the Word of God making sure of no contradictions, so I want to tread very lightly here.

In the scrolls found which were written by Enoch, he describes these fallen angels just as Genesis chapter 6 describes them. They looked upon the daughters of men and lusted for them and took them as their wives and bore children by them, 200 of them, according to the prophet Enoch. He refers to these fallen angels as "the Watchers". The Watchers also introduced things to mankind, such as astrology and the constellations, enchantments, root-cutting, the welding of metal to make swords and breastplates and ornaments. They taught them about the signs of the sun, the moon and the earth and knowledge of the clouds and of plants. Mankind embraced these teachings and they began to pervert God's way through the practice of black magic, fornication, bestiality and every evil thing. Because the evilness was so great and so dark, God had no choice except to flood the earth in order to kill off the evilness that had been taught to His people.

As a punishment, God banned this group of fallen angels to the abyss seen in God's Word. The children born to them, the giants, were evil and began eating flesh and drinking the blood of animals and humans, and committing indecent acts against them. They were destroyed in the flood, but their spirits lived on. According to Enoch, these evil spirits were banned to the earth and are not allowed to enter the presence of God; because according to God's design, they were not within His order. These are referred to as demons or evil spirits.

I know, beloved, this can be a lot to soak in, but I wanted to bring to light what's out there and what we are battling against in the realm of Spiritual Warfare as we study our enemy. I do encourage you to seek God as to what He would have you sift out or retain. I also want you to know that I would never mention or introduce anything to you that I did not feel had been validated already in God's Word!! Okay? So, don't throw me away yet, hang with me and sift out anything that you are not comfortable accepting.

To reveal the light of God's truth of peace, read Revelation 19:1 that is typed out for you, which also happens to be our memory verse for this week! Read through it several times out loud and let the enemy hear you and, most of all, let your soul hear it!

MEMORY VERSE

Revelation 19:1

"…Hallelujah! Salvation and glory and power belong to our God"

Studying Spiritual Warfare is in fact engaging in battle, beloved, and we must remember to stand in the truth of God's Word in the midst of it. The enemy will attack you with fear, threats, guilt, disputes and anything that will send your mind running from the truth. We must not give in to his schemes or his threats because we know Salvation, glory and power belongs to our God…Hallelujah!!!

This brings us to our Principle for today, beloved.

𝒫RINCIPLE

My Enemy Is Under My God's Feet

There is no foe who can overtake the child of God, because God is above all! This sends the enemy running, precious one, and one day your God and my God is going to run him right into the eternal lake of fire where he will stay for all eternity. Look up the following verses and note what you learn from each.

Genesis 14:19-20

_____

_____

Psalm 18:6-18

_____

_____

_____

Psalm 78:35

_____

_____

_____

Oh, beloved warrior, because your enemy is under God's feet, then the following is true:

LIFE APPLICATION

MY ENEMY HAS NO POWER OVER ME

In Spiritual Warfare the most vital truth that a warrior of God can remember is that He is over all, not the enemy. We are in the army of the Living God and you know what? WE WIN! There is no fear for those in the Kingdom of God…none. I want us to close our time together with our confession of truth. This time, I want you to write out your confession based on the truth you've learned or been reminded of about God. This is so important, beloved, so don't skip this part. Much love to you!

MY CONFESSION OF TRUTH

_____

_____

_____

_____

_____

_____

_____

_____

_____

_____

_____

Day Two

She was only 17 years old; she was her mama's youngest child. She had never given her mother any trouble, in fact, she sang in the children's choir at church. I led the church choir at the time and she was the epitome of a well-behaved child. She was loved and raised in church by a mother who was one of the godliest women I have ever met. Her mother was a praying woman, full of gentle strength and was so loving with her children. In her senior year of high school, the young woman took a turn in behavior that was immediately noticeable in the household, especially by her mother. Her dress began to change; her music and the decorations in her room all took a turn to the dark side. She began to withdraw from the light of her family and church. In desperation, her mother brought her in for counseling to the church. In God's providence, I was there that day and the presence of evil became very real to me. I came to know that it can be devastatingly powerful in the lives of people.

What began as a quiet counseling session soon erupted into noises unlike anything I had ever heard. When she was asked about Jesus, her whole demeanor changed and a scowling voice began to emerge and make its presence known. The presence threw the young woman down on the floor into convulsions and in a fit of rage. Her body was thrown around like a rag doll. It was obvious to all of us present that day that this was a demonic (evil) spirit and it had made its abode in the flesh of this young woman. It identified itself by name, which I will not write in order to avoid giving glory to Satan's kingdom. Every staff member joined in the praying, doing spiritual combat with a very powerful and dark force that refused to leave. With no other recourse, everyone in the room began to confess their sins in order to be clean vessels in which God could work. The Word of God was opened and the name of Jesus began to be proclaimed loudly and resolutely as Lord over all. After many hours of grueling intercessory prayer, the presence left.

The mother had no idea what had happened in the body of her daughter; she only knew that something was wrong. She had sensed oppression in the house for weeks, but didn't know what it was. Her daughter, although raised in church, had never accepted Christ as her Lord and Savior, but all that changed on this day. Praise the Lord! When she realized what happened, she surrendered her life to Jesus and asked Him to come in and be her Lord and Savior. She's now grown and married with children, loving the Lord with her life. I've since heard the same sound of evil coming from others who were possessed; the sound is undeniable if you've ever heard it. It's the darkest, most hopeless, angry sound, one could hear; a sound void of all life and all that is good. This was reality and it is reality today.

Spiritual Warfare is a universal problem for the unsaved and the saved alike, young and old. It matters not what you believe or don't believe; the truth of God's Word clearly reveals to us that the unseen realm exists and we are on one side or the other. It exists, beloved, and as we have seen, the opposing side is destructively powerful in destroying lives and holding them bondage. Praise God that at the mention of Jesus, demons must flee and the captive is set free. Every force that exists yields to His name, because of the authority of the God, Most High. We are victorious and safe under the blood of Jesus! So with that said, take time to pray and ask the Lord's blessings upon your study and for His protection as you do. We'll begin once you are finished.

Let's start off our study building a chart of truth regarding demons, evil spirits and fallen angels. Continue adding to our Adversary Chart on Satan. Whether they are one in the same, or father and sons, it doesn't really matter as long as we glean what God desires for us to glean and then combat accordingly. I want us to look at the demonic man that Jesus encountered. It is mentioned in two of the Gospels, so I want us to look at each account to make sure we get every detail. These passages are typed out for you at the end of today's lesson for your convenience. Read through each one and note what is happening. Take a colored pencil and mark every reference to the man by drawing a stick figure over each one with the color of your choice. Make a list of the man's life and how the demon affected him in the corresponding chart.

Mark 5:1-20 Demonic Man

Luke 8:27-39 Demonic Man

Turn to Matthew 8:28-34 where this same account is given and note anything new you did not see in the other two accounts. Matthew's account is much shorter than the others, but he does let us know that there were two demonic men.

_____

_____

_____

Could these men live normal lives being demon possessed? Why or why not?

_____

_____

Was their health affected? If so, how?

_____

_____

_____

How did Matthew describe these two men? What word did he use? What should this show us?

_____

_____

_____

Were others affected by these men who were demon possessed? If so, how?

_____

_____

_____

The Kingdom of Darkness affected this man on many levels? How was he changed and in what way was he empowered or weakened? List these effects in the appropriate column.

Weakened With	**Empowered With**
_____	_____
_____	_____
_____	_____
_____	_____

It's not something we usually think about when it comes to demonic possession, but we see that the demons gave great physical strength and capabilities to the body. Although he weakened his mind, the demon gave strength to the flesh. This is an important truth concerning Satan's realm;

he will always seek to strengthen the flesh. Turn in your Bible to Galatians 5:17 and note what you learn about the spirit and the flesh.

_____

_____

Why might Satan's Kingdom set out to strengthen our flesh? How would this help his cause?

_____

_____

It is the flesh that destroys the spirit, beloved, and thus it will be Satan's target to feed the flesh, so it will grow strong in order to take over the spirit of a person. This is why we do not war according to the flesh; the battle is against the spirit, and our spirit is a target. This is what attracts people to the occult world because it offers power to the flesh and freedom for which the flesh longs. The flesh will always seek to have power and control and, especially freedom, to do as it pleases. The flesh will never opt for boundaries, and its enemy will always be the spirit.

Let's go back through these same two passages in Luke and Mark, but this time draw a red cross over every reference to Jesus, including all pronouns. Once you are finished, make a list of all you learned about Jesus from your markings. There is a chart provided. Take your time, precious student!!!

Jesus
_____
_____
_____
_____
_____
_____
_____
_____

Did the demons recognize Jesus? If so, what did they know about Him?

_____

_____

Who was the higher authority between the demons and Jesus? Explain your answer based on what these verses tell us.

_____

_____

How was the man, who was possessed, described after Jesus freed him?

_____

_____

I was in Haiti a few years ago conducting a prayer conference with women. We had come in from a long, hot, tiring day of ministry and had sat down to eat some much needed food. I heard that sound, the sound void of life, angry and powerful. It was coming from the street in front of the mission compound where we were staying. I ran to the wall to look and there in the street was a woman with her clothes torn, hair disheveled, and ashes smeared all over her body. She did not have her senses about her and the demon threw her into fits out in the street. Some people passing by spit at her and hissed in disdain, while others fled in fear. She was violent, half-clothed and as a dead woman who was still a part of life. We see the same picture here in the life of these men and the one who had the "legion" of demons inside of him. But when Jesus came, they bowed the knee and obeyed Him; by coming out of Him and going into the swine. They needed permission to do that! Afterwards, the man was seen clothed and in his right mind sitting at the feet of Jesus.

In his right mind meant that his sanity had returned to him. What does this tell us about the power of demonic oppression? How can it manifest itself?

_____

_____

_____

_____

Evil spirits or demons can affect our lives in numerous ways, the greatest of these being the sanity of our minds. We are no longer under the control of what is good; therefore, our thoughts are tormented and confused. Like the ones we have read about today, they had no control over their actions because their minds were under the control of another. If the enemy can control the mind, he can defeat the spirit. This brings us to our principle today, beloved.

*P*RINCIPLE

THE KINGDOM OF DARKNESS GIVES STRENGTH TO OUR FLESH TO WEAKEN THE SPIRIT

Our spirit will always be Satan's challenge, his drive, and his target of destruction. But in order for Satan to do that, he will give strength to your flesh. He will empower it in order to use it as a weapon against the spirit man. Your flesh, beloved, is the most destructive of all weapons that Satan will use against you. We often live in fear of the spirit realm because we cannot see it; we know it is very powerful, however our real fear should be giving life to our flesh. As we journey through our study, we will go deeper into this truth and learn to live it and walk in the truth of it every day! I have laid a lot on you today, precious warrior, so I want to cut our time a little short, just so you can have time to soak these things in. Our goal will always be to strengthen our spirit and weaken our flesh. A good Bible study should do both! Read the principle out loud and follow through with your Life Application.

Principle: Because the Kingdom of Darkness gives strength to our flesh in order to weaken the spirit:

*L*IFE *A*PPLICATION

WE MUST STRENGTHEN THE SPIRIT TO WEAKEN THE FLESH

Our efforts must be to give life to the spirit at any cost. The more life we give to the spirit man, the more we will weaken the flesh. Let's close today with our confession of truth.

Confession of Truth

I am a child of God. The spirit of the living God dwells within me. My adversary seeks to destroy the life of the Spirit Who indwells me. I must die to my flesh and give it no opportunity to be fed.. I will give my flesh no strength today and I will guard myself against the attacks and schemes of the devil. There is no force that can overcome me because I belong to God.

I'm proud of you, precious student. Review your memory verse and we'll call it a day.

Mark 5:1-20

1. They came to the other side of the sea, into the country of the Gerasenes.

2. When He got out of the boat, immediately a man from the tombs with an unclean spirit met Him,

3. and he had his dwelling among the tombs. And no one was able to bind him anymore, even with a chain;

4. because he had often been bound with shackles and chains, and the chains had been torn apart by him and the shackles broken in pieces, and no one was strong enough to subdue him.

5. Constantly, night and day, he was screaming among the tombs and in the mountains, and gashing himself with stones.

6. Seeing Jesus from a distance, he ran up and bowed down before Him;

7. and shouting with a loud voice, he said, "What business do we have with each other, Jesus, Son of the Most High God? I implore You by God, do not torment me!"

8. For He had been saying to him, "Come out of the man, you unclean spirit!"

9. And He was asking him, "What is your name?" And he said to Him, "My name is Legion; for we are many."

10. And he began to implore Him earnestly not to send them out of the country.

11. Now there was a large herd of swine feeding nearby on the mountain.

12. The demons implored Him, saying, "Send us into the swine so that we may enter them."

13. Jesus gave them permission. And coming out, the unclean spirits entered the swine; and the herd rushed down the steep bank into the sea, about two thousand of them; and they were drowned in the sea.

14. Their herdsmen ran away and reported it in the city and in the country. And the people came to see what it was that had happened.

15. They came to Jesus and observed the man who had been demon-possessed sitting down, clothed and in his right mind, the very man who had had the "legion"; and they became frightened.

16. Those who had seen it described to them how it had happened to the demon-possessed man, and all about the swine.

17. And they began to implore Him to leave their region.

18. As He was getting into the boat, the man who had been demon-possessed was imploring Him that he might accompany Him.

19. And He did not let him, but He said to him, "Go home to your people and report to them what great things the Lord has done for you, and how He had mercy on you."

20. And he went away and began to proclaim in Decapolis what great things Jesus had done for him; and everyone was amazed.

Luke 8:27-39

27 And when He came out onto the land, He was met by a man from the city who was possessed with demons; and who had not put on any clothing for a long time, and was not living in a house, but in the tombs.

28 Seeing Jesus, he cried out and fell before Him, and said in a loud voice, "What business do we have with each other, Jesus, Son of the Most High God? I beg You, do not torment me."

29 For He had commanded the unclean spirit to come out of the man. For it had seized him many times; and he was bound with chains and shackles and kept under guard, and yet he would break his bonds and be driven by the demon into the desert.

30 And Jesus asked him, "What is your name?" And he said, "Legion"; for many demons had entered him.

31 They were imploring Him not to command them to go away into the abyss.

32 Now there was a herd of many swine feeding there on the mountain; and the demons implored Him to permit them to enter the swine. And He gave them permission.

33 And the demons came out of the man and entered the swine; and the herd rushed down the steep bank into the lake and was drowned.

34 When the herdsmen saw what had happened, they ran away and reported it in the city and out in the country.

35 The people went out to see what had happened; and they came to Jesus, and found the man from whom the demons had gone out,

sitting down at the feet of Jesus, clothed and in his right mind; and they became frightened.

36 Those who had seen it reported to them how the man who was demon-possessed had been made well.

37 And all the people of the country of the Gerasenes and the surrounding district asked Him to leave them, for they were gripped with great fear; and He got into a boat and returned.

38 But the man from whom the demons had gone out was begging Him that he might accompany Him; but He sent him away, saying,

39 "Return to your house and describe what great things God has done for you." So he went away, proclaiming throughout the whole city what great things Jesus had done for him.

Day Three

The end of living is the beginning of survival. For so many living in the world today, there is no living, only survival; survival to get through each day, to pay the next bill, to get up in the morning and go to work, to face accusers, to start over, to go for their next cancer treatment, to make that necessary phone call, to live with the pain others have caused, to live another day in a prison cell, to take the next breath, to lay down and sleep without fear or just to eat the next meal. The eyes of the natural reveal both good and bad. But the spiritual eye is needed to understand and fight the battle for life that is taking place. Because of this, spiritual blindness has focused in on what it can see, pain, suffering, and every other thing that brings us low and into the valley of only survival. The battle for the need to see is very great and many struggle to climb up the wall, the wall of what they believe is understanding struggling. They want to get to a place where they can catch their breath or see from a different perspective, hoping this will see them through. The reality is we will never see with the eyes of our flesh what the spirit is doing. Let me share a story that is so powerful and has been preserved for hundreds of years.

A Grandfather from the Cherokee Nation was talking with his grandson.
"A fight is going on inside me," he said to the boy. "It is a terrible fight between two wolves."

The young grandson listened intently.

"One wolf is evil, unhappy, and ugly: He is anger, envy, war, greed, selfishness, sorrow, regret, guilt, resentment, inferiority/superiority, false pride, coarseness, and arrogance. He spreads lies, deceit, fear, hatred, blame, scarcity, poverty, and divisiveness."
"The other wolf is beautiful and good: He is friendly, joyful, loving, worthy, serene, humble, kind, benevolent, just, fair, empathetic, generous, honest, compassionate, grateful, brave, and inspiring, resting wholeheartedly in deep vision beyond ordinary wisdom."

The Grandfather continued; "This same fight is going on inside you and inside all human beings as well."

The grandson paused in deep reflection and recognition of what his grandfather had just said. Then he finally cried out deeply; "Grandfather, which wolf will win this horrific war"?

"The Grandfather replied, "The wolf that you feed. That wolf will surely win!"

We learned this in our time of study on Day Two, beloved. Satan's kingdom will always seek to give life to the flesh in order to bring death to the Spirit. We want to continue looking at the effects of the forces of wickedness that are in the heavenly places and the world forces of darkness that exist. I believe that these two forces make for us a distinction between the fallen angels and the demons or evil spirits. Take time to pray before you start your study and we will begin. We want to make sure we can recognize forces that are contrary to God. To help us, let's look at the following verses that show us what powers evil forces can have and how they can affect the lives of people and who they obey, etc. We want to take notice of how they entice and what they entice people to do or not do. How do they affect our emotions, our lives, our thoughts, etc.? As you look up each verse, note what you learn from each and answer any questions that may follow.

Judges 9:23-24

_____

_____

I Samuel 16:14-23 & 18:10

_____

_____

I King 22:20-23

_____

_____

Job 4:12-21

_____

_____

Hosea 4:12 & 5:4

_____

_____

Matthew 12:43-45

_____

_____

Mark 1:23-26 (Note where this man was and when the evil spirit cried out.)

_____

_____

This demonic man was in the synagogue, the place of worship. What does this tell us?

_____

_____

Mark 7:25-29

_____

_____

Mark 9:16-29

_____

_____

Luke 11:11-13

_____

_____

Acts 19:13-20

_____

_____

_____

Acts 16:16-18

_____

_____

Acts 5:16

_____

_____

James 3:11-18

_____

_____

I know this has been a good bit to look up, beloved, but we must be informed before we can be prepared! Amen? What a trooper you are!!! You go, girl!!!

*P*RINCIPLE

EVIL SPIRITS CAN BE DESTRUCTIVE IN EVERY AREA OF ONE'S LIFE

As we have seen, evil spirits or demonic spirits can take our health from us. It can raise up a spirit of anger, jealousy, and malice. It can deceive us through words that are misleading. They can cause us to have bouts of uncontrolled bodily functions, like the young boy. We know that they can attack any age, young or old, male or female. They manipulate our emotions and they dispel their opinions in public places, such as the church, etc. With their presence can come dread and fear and we can physically sometimes feel their presence, as Job did. They can hurt our bodies with physical pain by mauling us; they can also cause us to cut ourselves or throw us into areas of danger, such as fire or water to try and drown us. Beloved, these are serious life-threatening attacks. We must be aware of them, at all times, so when we encounter them we will know with what force we are dealing.

This usually brings a flood of questions... What are we to do? Are we to approach evil spirits and call them out? Can evil spirits indwell someone who is a Christian? These are all pertinent questions, precious warrior, and I want to show you just a couple of verses to help us get a better understanding of our response to evil spirits. We will cover this in more detail when we get into our Weapons of Warfare. I do want to touch briefly on any confusion that may have arisen in your heart and to help settle any doubts or uncertainty you might have. Look up and read the following verses and note what you see regarding our role and our protection against evil spirits, if any.

I John 4:1

_____

_____

I Timothy 4:1-8 (Pay close attention to what we can do and what it will do for us.)

_____

_____

Matthew 12:24-29

_____

_____

Turn to your Word Windows Section located in the back of your study and locate the meaning for the word *"Strong"* as used here in Matthew. Record your findings in the space provided.

Strong

_____

_____

In this passage who do you think the strong man is?

_____

_____

The Pharisees accused Jesus of casting out demons by the power of Satan (Beelzebul), himself. Jesus went on to teach that this was not possible and would not make sense; it's like going to war against yourself! Who would be the winner in that? He went on to explain that before someone could come in and plunder the house of the strong man, they had to first bind the strong man. Jesus is able, beloved!

Based on this story, do you think Satan would be able to come in and take over your life (your house) if Jesus were the owner, the strong man? Satan cannot overtake Jesus and before someone or something can overtake your house, they have to be able to bind the strong man! This brings us to our Life application. Read today's Principle out loud and then follow it with the Life Application. It will set your feet to dancing!!!

Principle: EVIL SPIRITS CAN BE DESTRUCTIVE IN EVERY AREA OF ONE'S LIFE

My Life Application Is...

BUT THEY CANNOT TAKE OVER THE HOUSE THAT BELONGS TO THE STRONG MAN

There is no fear for the house, the temple that belongs to the Strong Man, beloved! If the demons and evil spirits had to submit to Jesus' authority, then do you think He would allow them to go in and occupy what belongs to Him? Never! Do you remember the demonic man who had a "legion" of demons living inside of him? Didn't they have to ask Jesus' permission to go into the swine? What belongs to Jesus will never go to another, beloved! Never! I want you to write the words: JESUS IS THE STRONG MAN OF THIS HOUSE, in the space provided. Read it aloud several times over!

_____

_____

They are *"shoutin"* words to this warrior! Whenever the enemy comes against you and attacks you with fear, I want you to say these words out loud so he can hear them: JESUS IS THE STRONG MAN OF THIS HOUSE! And watch him flee and when he goes, fear goes with him.

In Jesus' prayer before His crucifixion in John 17, Jesus proclaims to the Father that all that He had given to Him, no one was able to snatch them out of His hand! God wants us to know fully that we are absolutely safe forevermore in His hands and in the hands of His Son.

This is our wonderful confession of truth for today.

My Confession of Truth

I confess that I am a child of the living God. Jesus lives in me through the Holy Spirit and therefore, I have been declared as the temple of the Lord God Almighty. He has ownership of me and no one is able to overtake what belongs to Him. I am His house and Jesus is in the house! Not only is He in the house, but Jesus is the Strong Man of this house. No one can take the house from the Strong Man! Jesus, You will keep me from the enemy. I will have no fear because God's Word is truth.

Confessions of truth are crucial for weaving truth into the fabric of our lives; it gives us a new spiritual wardrobe to wear! Remember that faith comes by hearing and hearing by the Word of God. It is necessary to hear truth, so it is important to read it aloud. Let's close out our time together today by writing out our memory verse for this week in the space provided. Make sure you include the scripture reference. And in case I haven't told you today, I am so very proud of you. As I write these words, I am praying for you and the lives that you will impact as a result of your warfare.

MEMORY VERSE

_____

_____

_____

_____

Day Four

If I were to say to you, give me a high five with your left hand and say aloud your five unseen resistances, could you do it? I bet you could! I pray you've been saying these over and over again until they are engraved permanently upon your heart. Truth repeated will sear itself in until it has imprinted the mark it was intended to leave. God's Word leaves His fingerprints all over our lives because it is living, active, and sharper than any two-edged sword. The more we study God's Word, the more alive the Word becomes in us; the more alive it is in us, the more the world will see it. God's Word was never meant to be dead in us, or idling, waiting for a chance to act! So let me start you off with a big question, beloved. How's your engine running? Or is it running?

With that said, let's stop and pray and ask God's blessings on our study and for His hand to open our eyes so we can behold wonderful truths from His Word today. Today, I want us to look at a powerful scene with God and our adversary, the devil, found in Zechariah chapter 3. Read through these verses that are typed out for you and as you do, note what is happening in this scene and where it is taking place. Note your insights on the chart provided for you.

Zechariah 3:1-5

1. *Then he showed me Joshua the high priest standing before the angel of the LORD, and Satan standing at his right hand to accuse him.*
2. *The LORD said to Satan, "The LORD rebuke you, Satan! Indeed, the LORD who has chosen Jerusalem rebuke you! Is this not a brand plucked from the fire?"*
3. *Now Joshua was clothed with filthy garments and standing before the angel.*
4. *He spoke and said to those who were standing before him, saying, "Remove the filthy garments from him." Again he said to him, "See, I have taken your iniquity away from you and will clothe you with festal robes."*
5. *Then I said, "Let them put a clean turban on his head." So they put a clean turban on his head and clothed him with garments, while the angel of the LORD was standing by.*

Describing the Scene

_____

_____

_____

_____

_____

_____

_____

Take a colored a pencil and mark every reference to Satan in this passage in the same way as we have been doing. Once you've finished, write out any insights you gathered from marking the text.

Satan

_____

_____

_____

_____

What do we see Satan doing in this scene and to whom?

_____

_____

Let's read through this passage once more, only this time marking every reference to Joshua, the High Priest, by drawing a circle around each using the color of your choice. Make a list of everything you saw from your markings. Remember to ask your questions: Who, What, When, Where, Why and How? Write out your insights on the Joshua Chart.

Joshua, the High Priest

_____

_____

_____

_____

_____

_____

Was Joshua a servant of God? Explain your answer.

_____

_____

How was Joshua, the High Priest dressed? Describe his clothing.

_____

_____

The High Priest was a position that was given as a birthright, which was chosen by God. It was a service appointed by God to the tribe of Levi. The Levites were responsible for tending to the House of the Lord and all the duties that come with the service. It was a life-long calling and one that was held in high esteem. The most prominent position was that of the High Priest. There was only one High Priest and when he died another took his place. Turn to the following verses and note the attire of the High Priest according to God's plan.

Exodus 28:1-4

_____

_____

_____

To see that Joshua, the High Priest was in filthy garments is odd, isn't it? What do you think this might mean?

_____

Turn to your Word Windows Section and locate the meaning for the word "*Filthy.*" Record your findings in the space provided for you.

Filthy

_____

_____

Based on the word meaning for "filthy," what do you think these filthy rags represent?

_____

_____

Turn to Isaiah 61:10 and note how God has clothed His children.

_____

_____

Just as God had ordained the clothing for His servant, so He has for all His servants. The servant of the Lord has designated clothing, beloved, and they are by God's design. Too often we want to come to God to be saved from a situation, a lifestyle, an addiction, a past, etc... but we want to continue to clothe ourselves in fleshly garments. Joshua was the High Priest and yet, he was clothed in filthy rags. I believe we see such beautiful and powerful symbolism here. Turn to the following passage of scripture and note what you see about filthy rags.

_____

_____

Our sin and even our very best are as filthy rags compared to the Lord. In other words, we can never be good enough for God. These are hard words to take in, but true, precious one. God loved us too much to leave us in our filthy rags of failure so He sent us Jesus, that He might clothe us with robes of righteousness as we read in Isaiah 61:10. If we remain in our filthy rags, they will only serve as a reminder of our guilt, failure and inability to be "good enough." They are the banner of shame and failure for each and every one of us if we keep them about us. Think with me on these things as you answer the following questions.

Where was Satan positioned in regard to Joshua?

_____

_____

Satan was standing at the right hand of Joshua. The right hand was the symbol of power or authority. What symbolism does this give us? What does this tell you about Satan?

_____

_____

Satan will stand to remind us and God of how unworthy we are. Satan will parade us and seek to clothe us with our failures as a constant reminder. What are you wearing, precious warrior? What place has Satan taken in your life? Where we allow him to go will determine what he will be able to do. In Joshua's life he had assumed the place of authority, the place of influence and guidance. This brings us to our Principle today.

*P*RINCIPLE

SATAN WILL SEEK THE PLACE OF INFLUENCE IN MY LIFE

Satan will seek the place of influence in your life in order to condemn you before God. He will cunningly scheme with the intent of assuming the place to the right of you, precious warrior, the place of authority, the place of influence. If he can get to that place, he can whisper to the heart and infiltrate the mind of God's child in order to turn them away from God. He will try and present you before God in "filthy rags"! He is an accuser and has been from the beginning. It's the filthy rags that Satan wants to keep us clothed in, by removing our Royal Robes. Your robe is your identity and who you are in Christ. If he can cause us to stumble, to fall, to sin, or to turn away from the path God wants us to take, then, he has woven for us unrighteous robes.

Satan is a master weaver of destruction, beloved, and we must not be ignorant of his intentions. If Satan can't get us to fall, if he can't weave a new garment of unrighteousness for us to wear, then, he will pull out our rags of the past. Recognizing these garments is the first step to overcoming. What are your rags from the past, precious one? What is it that the enemy will pull out from your closet of failure? List these out as God brings them to your mind.

RAGS FROM MY CLOSET OF FAILURE

_____
_____
_____
_____
_____
_____
_____
_____
_____

Satan desires to accuse us before God with the rags of our failure. Another scheme Satan desires is to blind us into weaving our own robes of self-righteousness which will always come up short. Satan wants us to come up short when we stand before God! But we must overcome, beloved! Look up the following verses of scripture and note what you learn from each.

II Corinthians 5:21

_____

_____

Philippians 3:1-9

_____

_____

I Corinthians 6:9-11

_____

_____

Isaiah 44:22

_____

_____

Micah 7:19

_____

_____

I John 1:9 (Many are familiar with this one!)

_____

_____

Oh, precious warrior of God's army, we must gird ourselves with the truth of who we are in Jesus Christ. Whatever your rags are, you need to burn them in the memory of your heart as an offering unto the Lord, because He has forgotten them. He has poured them out into the deepest part of the sea and you are forgiven, forevermore. Don't cast off the royal robes Christ died to give you; allowing the enemy to trample underfoot the mercies of God. Learn to recognize that God clothed you in Jesus with robes of holiness and splendor, but it is your responsibility to adorn what He has given to you. Let's read our Principle aloud and then follow it with our Life Application today.

Principle: Because Satan will seek the place of influence in my life:

LIFE APPLICATION

HE MUST FIND IT ALREADY OCCUPIED

When the enemy comes to our place of influence, he should find it already occupied with truth. We often fall prey to his destructive vices because we have emptied the Lord from the place of authority, of power and influence and have replaced it with something or someone else. The Lord will never leave His post, beloved, so it is up to us not to try and replace Him. When we do this, we hang out a vacancy sign for Satan that says, "Stay here," when the sign should read, "No Vacancies." I want us to read aloud our confession of truth for today.

My Confession of Truth

I proclaim loudly and courageously, fully believing that in Jesus I have been completely justified and made righteous in the eyes of God. I was born anew into the royal family of Heaven and as a child of the King, I have been robed with spotless garments of splendor. I will dress no longer in earthly rags because of who I am. I will not listen to the enemy because all that he says is a lie. There is no truth in him; therefore, I will give him no place of influence in my life. I will allow no one, or nothing, to occupy the place of authority and influence, but the truth of God's Word and His Holy Spirit Who dwells within me. My past is forgiven and my future is set and I will press on with Jesus all my days.

We must learn the powerful, life-giving benefit of proclaiming truth out loud! It is the war cry of every child of God, beloved, and cry it aloud, we must. This is where victory is declared for the enemy to hear and it will drown out the roar of the lion! Praise the Lord today with me for lips to declare truth and praise unto Him! One way to help us retain the truths we've learned this week is to go back and revisit them. Write them out by hand. Let's take time to do that now by looking back at our Principles and Life Applications and record them in the chart on the corresponding day.

OUR WEEK IN REVIEW

Day One

Principle:
Life Application:

Day Two

Principle:
Life Application:

Day Three

Principle:
Life Application:

Day Four

Principle:
Life Application:

How wonderful truth is, precious one. You will learn truth is our armor and without it we are vulnerable for attack and prone to injury. I want to close out our day with some Personal Evaluation time. Read the following and answer as God leads and reveals truth to your heart. Much love to you! I want to encourage you to stay the course with me! We have the hard truths behind us and now comes the armor and so much more; I don't want you to miss any of it. It does no good to study the enemy only; we must learn how to defend and stand our ground if we are ever to live the life of the victor, rather than the victim.

Personal Evaluation

Are there any areas of your life that you have allowed Satan to occupy?

_____

_____

Have you put your enemy under God's feet or do you feel like you are under the enemy's feet?

_____

_____

_____

Do you know who your Strong Man is? Who is the Strong Man of your house? Do you feel that your house (life) is being plundered? What must you do?

_____

_____

_____

What are you clothing yourself with every day? Explain.

_____

_____

_____

Are you guarding the doors of your life? If so, how? If not, what areas do you need to protect?

_____

_____

_____

_____

Session Notes

LESSON FOUR

Piercing the Darkness

Piercing the Darkness

Day One

An estimated 100 million Christians worldwide suffer interrogation, arrest, and even death for their faith in Jesus Christ, with millions more facing discrimination and alienation. The isolated communist country of North Korea has been ranked as the No. 1 persecutor of Christians eight years in a row on Open Doors' World Watch List, an organization dedicated to support and strengthen believers in the world's most difficult areas. They recognize North Korea as the worst place on earth to be a Christian, primarily because there are between 40,000 to 60,000 Christians who are in labor camps right now, simply because of their faith in Jesus Christ. It's the world's largest prison. Their founder describes North Korea in this way: *"It feels like North Korea is covered in a thick spiritual layer of fog. Inside this country there is a depressive atmosphere."* North Korean dictator, Kim Jong-II, is in fact an absolutely horrific tyrant to the Christians in North Korea.

All of its citizens, but especially Christians, are denied any opportunity to practice their belief by studying the Bible, engaging in worship, or evangelization of any kind. If they are caught, a labor camp awaits them. If they have children or grandparents, they can be thrown into a labor camp as well. Most of the citizens of North Korea believe in the leadership of their country. They are like gods to them. They have to bow down to their statues. The leaders are worshipped everywhere. No doubt that the Spiritual Warfare raging over this country is profound. Living in a country where we are free to worship the Lord as we see fit, it is difficult for us to wrap our heads around such a life. I can't imagine having to bow to a statue of one of our leaders every time I pass by. The spiritual darkness that enshrouds these lands seems to be impenetrable for the church and the devoted followers of Christ who are in hiding this very hour for their safety and the safety of their families.

North Korea is only one place in the world where persecution of Christians is rampant. The spiritual battle in progress is fierce and relentless. There is evil and cruelty, depression and sickness. Lives are being destroyed by superstition and ignorance, brutality and pain. God, the Father, the Son, and the Holy Spirit, are in constant battle against it. . They are for life and against death, for love and against hate, for hope and against despair. They are for Heaven and against hell. Knowing and believing that is no neutral ground, we, who belong to God's Kingdom, have no choice except to be in the battle! Awareness of the battle, and warring in on the front lines, are two different truths altogether, though the two are linked. Having identified the existence of the Spiritual Battle that rages continuously and having examined the enemy and his army, we now turn our attention to our role in the battle and how to stand firm against our enemy as God has directed. We were not created in weakness, but in power and might by the hand of the Living God! Pray before you begin, beloved!

Hold up your left hand and recite the five unseen resistances that come against us. Once you do this, write them out on the picture provided of the corresponding finger as way of review. We want these unseen resistances fresh before us, precious one, because of what we will be studying. You're going to learn how to combat each one of these resistances throughout the rest of our study time. We are headed down Victory Lane! We must never forget our five unseens, beloved!

<u>MY FIVE UNSEEN RESISTANCES</u>

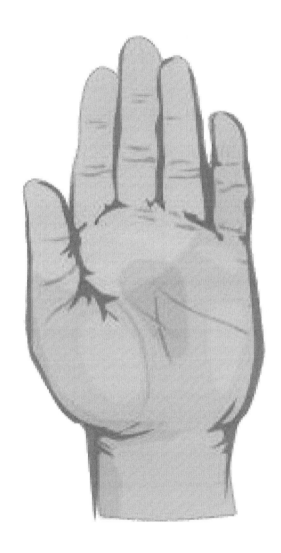

From our study so far, do you believe these unseen resistances are real? Explain why or why not, based on what you have learned and seen so far.

_____

_____

Has your thinking changed toward the enemy? Has it changed regarding Spiritual Battle? If so, explain how it has changed and why.

_____

_____

_____

Our main text of study today will be II Corinthians 10:3-5. For your convenience, it's typed out for you following this paragraph. Although this is not a new passage for us in our study, I want us to look freshly at it today and zero in on the verses we have not reviewed as of yet. Take it in and let this passage sink deeply into your soul. . Write out your thoughts concerning this passage and note what our role in Spiritual battle might be according to these verses.

MY ROLE IN BATTLE

II Corinthians 10:3-5

3. For though we walk in the flesh, we do not war according to the flesh,
4. for the weapons of our warfare are not of the flesh, but divinely powerful for the destruction of fortresses.
5. We are destroying speculations and every lofty thing raised up against the knowledge of God, and we are taking every thought captive to the obedience of Christ.

I want us to go back through this passage of scripture and this time, mark every reference to the person in warfare. These will be the pronouns "we" and "our." Mark these by drawing a circle around each one with the color of your choosing. Once you have marked every reference, write out what you learn about the warrior in spiritual battle.

The Warrior of Spiritual Battle

_____

_____

_____

_____

_____

According to this passage of scripture, where are our weapons not found?

_____

Since our battle is not against flesh and blood, our weapons must not be of the flesh. Because they are not of the flesh, what are they able to do? Write out the power of these weapons.

_____

_____

_____

_____

I believe with my whole heart that we lose many battles because we are either fighting the wrong battle or we are warring with the wrong weapons. We are given such powerful truths in this treasure of Scripture. It is absolutely vital for us to understand. We must recognize the power that God has given us to battle in the Spiritual realm. He would never leave us without the things needed for victory. We are given five power- packed truths about our Spiritual weaponry. I want to write these five things out for you, beloved, so we can be united in our terminology throughout the rest of our study. In this passage of scripture, we are given a description of our weapons.

OUR SPIRITUAL WEAPONRY

1. DIVINELY POWERFUL
2. WILL DESTROY FORTRESSES
3. WILL DESTROY SPECULATIONS
4. WILL DESTROY EVERY LOFTY THING RAISED UP AGAINST GOD
5. CAPTIVATE EVERY THOUGHT TO OBEY JESUS

Our weapons are no ordinary weapons, beloved, because they are divinely powerful! Because they are divinely powerful, we must understand that these weapons cannot be found within our flesh, our own abilities, strengths, talents or resources. They are found within the spirit realm. The battle is fought within the spirit realm, so its weapons are also discovered in the spirit realm. This is a most valuable truth, beloved warrior, and our hearts must be drawn to this truth and we must train ourselves by it. Let me give you some food for thought by asking you these questions, "When you feel you are under attack, what weapons do you reach for first? What is your first reaction when you feel you are being attacked"?

_____

_____

_____

How do you respond when someone hurts you? When you feel as though someone is out to hurt you or someone you love such as your children, a relative or friend, how do you respond?

_____

_____

Before we can pick up the weapons that are divinely powerful, we must acknowledge what the wrong weapons are so we can distinguish between the two! We often cannot, or will not, take up God's weapons to do battle because our hands are already full of our own. I've lost countless battles because I used weapons that were fleshly and only powerful to destroy God's name, my testimony, and the lives of others. I want us to understand what (Paul) the writer means by the terminology **"divinely powerful."** Let's look up these two words in our Word Windows Section and record their meanings in the space provided.

Divinely

_____

_____

_____

Powerful

_____

_____

_____

Based on your word studies, what do you think it means to have weapons that are "divinely powerful"? Describe these weapons in the light of their words' meanings.

Divinely Powerful Weapons

_____

_____

_____

Spiritual Warfare is engaging the unseen; therefore, the weapons we engage in battle with are unseen as well. If we are reaching for something we can lay hold of in the physical realm, we cannot do battle in the spiritual realm. This brings us to our Principle for today.

*P*RINCIPLE

SPIRITUAL WEAPONS ARE NECESSARY TO DO SPIRITUAL BATTLE

I think we can understand that the battle is a spiritual battle, but we continue trying to war with the weapons of the flesh. Flesh can only fight the flesh, beloved; it cannot fight in spiritual battles. I want us to look at some scriptures that will help validate this truth more. Spiritual Warfare is not an activity in your life where you can have victory if you are armed with the wrong weaponry. Look up the following verses and note what you learn about Spiritual Warfare and any weapons that are mentioned. Note the victories and how they are obtained.

Isaiah 54:16-17

_____

_____

Isaiah 51:19-23

_____

_____

_____

I Samuel 17:39-50

_____

_____

_____

Isaiah 22:8-11

_____

_____

_____

II Corinthians 6: 2-10

_____

_____

I Chronicles 29:10-13

_____

_____

All through the Word of God is woven this same truth: God is mighty to save, not man! God is the Mighty Warrior, not man. With God, all things are possible and with Him, there is nothing that is impossible! Amen? O that God would prick your hearts with this truth today concerning your weaponry. Are you losing a battle right now in your life, beloved? Then, check your weapons. You will not win against a spiritual enemy apart from spiritual weapons. I want you to read through our Principle and then, follow it by reading through our Life Application for today.

Principle: Because Spiritual Weapons Are Necessary To Do Spiritual Battle

LIFE APPLICATION

I MUST LAY DOWN MY WEAPONS OF THE FLESH

We must surrender before we can win, precious friend; surrender our own weapons and renounce their power and ability. They cannot help us and they will fail us every time. There is no victory in the flesh or anything that comes from the flesh. This is just the tip of what we will be learning about our spiritual weapons of battle. I want to share with you our memory verse for today. I've typed it out for you so take a few minutes and read over it several times, helping to seal it in your heart like the priceless treasure it is.

MEMORY VERSE

Deuteronomy 3:24

'O Lord GOD, You have begun to show Your servant Your greatness and Your strong hand; for what god is there in heaven or on earth who can do such works and mighty acts as Yours?

I pray that you can agree with this verse and that God has begun to show you His greatness and His strong hand. God has a strong hand, and in that hand is deliverance from, and victory over, every foe, every situation, every thought, every power, every army, and every force!

Let's close our time together today by reading aloud our confessions of truth. Read it aloud and let the enemy hear you! Much love for you, mighty warrior! See you on Day Two!

MY CONFESSION OF TRUTH

I confess that Lord, You are mighty to save. There is no weapon that is formed against me that can prosper and every word spoken against me You will cause to fail. Your hand is Strong and Powerful for the destruction of every evil thing that seeks to harm me or my family. My weapons are not my own but they are divinely powerful because they are of You. Your weapons can tear down every fortress. They can bring down every speculation that raises itself up against You, O Lord, and Your weapons can take captive every thought that doesn't please You.

Because of my spiritual weapons, I am powerful, I am not weak. I am able to tame my mind and break free from any fortress that has walled me in. I confess that my flesh is unable to fight in spiritual battles and I must take up the weapons given to me by You. I am not without hope and I cannot lose the battle warred in the spirit because I am Your child.

Day Two

I remember stepping off the plane after 18 hours of flying and layovers. I was on the other side of God's world so very far from home and all that was familiar. The hills of Japan had captivated my heart from the view the Lord allowed me to have from my plane window. Surely, this is what God must see every day as He commands the sun to show itself strong upon the volcanic country of the Japanese people. I believe it's with a broken heart that He does so as only about 1% are Christians there. I knew God had sent me to these people and I had prepared spiritually as best as I knew how, but nothing could have prepared me for what I encountered when I arrived. As soon as the plane began to make its descent, the excitement stirring inside of me turned to a dull gnawing pain in the deepest part of my abdomen. It was not from a physical ailment, although it was a very real pain, but it was something greater than just a tummy ache or nerves. I felt heaviness in my body, causing every moment to become laborious... I thought, "Maybe this is what jet-lag is," as this was the first time I had traveled across the international dateline.

There seemed to be darkness and gloom over the people. A literal pressure gripped my heart that I could hardly endure. Our entire group was on edge and, at times, at odds with one another for no visible reason. Not knowing what I had come up against, I began to pray, asking the Father to help restore my physical condition and to protect me and those traveling with me. I did not speak of this to anyone in my group, only to the Lord. During my two-week stay, the Lord began to open my eyes and allow me to see why this emptiness was so thick upon Japan. The Japanese people are very kind, intelligent, industrious and giving. They also worship idols and even offer food and drink at the headstones of their dead loved ones. Most Japanese homes have shrines with an idol of Buddha in their home in keeping with the traditions of their ancestors. There are Buddhist temples strategically located so the people can come and offer their prayers or breathe in incense as a token of cleansing and receiving help or blessings. Idols are sold in all the gift shops and worshipping Buddha is clearly a way of life for these people. I understood what I was feeling, spiritual oppression. This was the first time I had physically felt spiritual oppression on this level. It was very real, it was very dark and it was difficult to minister under the strain of such opposition.

Exodus 10:21 tells us; *Then the LORD said to Moses, "Stretch out your hand toward the sky, that there may be **darkness** over the land of Egypt, even a **darkness** which may be felt."* There is darkness, beloved, that can be felt yet, not seen. I have since that time experienced it on numerous occasions in other countries or cities, in public places, and from individuals. During my time in Japan, I had not experienced Spiritual Warfare firsthand so I did not know how to war according to the Spirit, other than to pray when I was in need and trust in God. Although this is a vital part to Spiritual Warfare, there is more needed to war a good fight. I want us to war a good fight, beloved, and know how to stand our ground. We need to excel spiritually, even when we come into areas of great darkness where we cannot sense God's presence because the enemy is so strong. God's Word is very clear to us regarding these encounters and with His help, we'll learn how to defend against the enemy. Take your time to pray, precious student, and then, we will begin our journey today in God's Word.

Job 12:25 says, *"They grope in darkness with no light."* We are not to grope in the darkness like those who have not come into the light. Today, I want us to continue looking at our weaponry and how we are to use it according to God's design. Let's begin by reading through our portion of scripture from Day One's study, II Corinthians 10:3-5. As way of review, I want us to write out these verses to help solidify them in our hearts and minds. I have given you space to do this, beloved student!

II Corinthians 10:3-5

3. _____

_____.

4. _____

_____.

5. _____

_____

_____

What do we see in verse 4 that our weapons are? (Fill in the blank.)

Divinely _____

Paul spoke of this to his son in the Lord, Timothy. Knowing that the Lord had given them these weapons that were divinely powerful, he admonished Timothy concerning the battle. Look up the following verses and note what Paul is telling Timothy in these passages regarding warfare.

I Timothy 1:18

_____

II Timothy 2:3

_____

_____

Paul was telling Timothy that he had been given all that was necessary to war a good war. It was up to Timothy to make that decision to be a good soldier. The Lord wants us to be good soldiers so we can fight a good fight! Knowing the heart of God concerning this is motivation enough for His children. He's given us spiritual weapons that are divinely powerful to destroy and to take the enemy captive so we can be the good soldiers He intends for us to be. Today, we want to focus on the divine power to destroy fortresses and speculations that are raised against us because of the very knowledge of God. Our enemy has weapons that destroy all that is holy, but our weapons destroy all that is evil. So, to understand what a fortress is, I want us to locate the meaning of this word in the Word Windows Section. Write down your insights in the space given.

Fortresses

_____

_____

In light of your word study, what do you think it might mean to encounter a fortress on a spiritual plane?

_____

_____

Have you ever encountered a fortress in your life? If so, explain.

_____

_____

_____

Why do you think God gave us this divine power?

_____

_____

God can easily come down in a cloud or pillar of fire to destroy everything that comes against us. In a time of need, He can tear down every fortress erected against us; instead, He gave *us* the power to accomplish this. "Why" is the question? Look up the following verses and take note of what you learn about each that might be insight as to why God instilled His power within us.

II Corinthians 3:5

_____

_____

II Corinthians 4:7

_____

_____

II Corinthians 13:3

_____

_____

Psalm 110:2

_____

_____

Isaiah 41:14-16

_____

_____

I Corinthians 2:5

_____

_____

Jeremiah 1:10

_____

_____

One more so hang in there! What a trooper you are…

Hebrews 11:30

_____

_____

God longs for us to believe in Him, to know His power and to trust in it for everything. God wants to be our continual source, but He wants to be our *only* source. This is how God builds our faith, precious one, and this is how He also gains the glory and receives all the credit. He created us weak and unable to defend ourselves against the spiritual forces because it is *His* battle and *He* is the contender. We are the weapons He uses to contend with, beloved, and through us He is mighty and powerful against every foe! This brings us to our Principle for today.

*P*RINCIPLE

SPIRITUAL WEAPONS BRING GLORY TO GOD IN BATTLE

This is a good test for us when we are fighting in the battles of life. Who is getting the glory? Whose strength is being seen, God's or mine? Whose plan is being followed, God's or mine? Whose weapons am I using, the Lord's or mine? Why am I fighting, for God or for me? Am I defending the Lord's name or my name? These questions have saved me from many fleshly battles! In the fleshly battles, beloved, God gets no glory and we will surely fail. Read the following verse from Isaiah and write down what you think this might mean in light of our topic of study today. I've typed out this verse for you.

Isaiah 9:2

"The people who walk in darkness Will see a great light; Those who live in a dark land, The light will shine on them."

My Thoughts

Spiritual battles are fought against the forces of darkness and the areas they are trying to occupy or even remain in. We can battle for ourselves, for our children, our family members, our friends, our church, and even for territories such as the country of Japan. No matter the size of the battlefield, the goal in warfare for God's children is always the same, that those in the darkness may "see a great light," the One Who is light.

Principle: Because Spiritual Weapons bring glory to God...

LIFE APPLICATION

LIGHT CAN SHINE IN DARKNESS

Genesis 1:3&4 teaches us that God created the light first and He saw that it was good and separated it from the darkness. God has made a clear distinction between light and darkness in the physical realm as a reminder for us in the spiritual realm. Just as there is a distinction between light and darkness in the world, we can also see this is true in the unseen world. When we lay down our weapons of the flesh and surrender the flesh as God's captive then, and only then, can we take up the weapons that are divinely powerful to shine the light of God in the land of darkness. What are your weapons of light, beloved? How are you separating the light from the darkness? Every time we war in the Spirit with those divine weapons, we are pouring forth light into the places of darkness. Take a few minutes and write out your memory verse in the space provided for you. Include your scripture reference.

Memory Verse

_____

_____

_____

_____

Scripture memorization is awesome in the life of a believer. You are building your arsenal, beloved, and you will have it in the day of battle. I'm so proud of you. Let's close with our confession of truth for today.

My Confession of Truth

Lord, I confess before every spiritual force of wickedness in the heavenly places and before every force of darkness that You are Lord of all and You are powerful over all. I confess before the rulers, the powers and before the devil, himself that You reign victorious and there is no weapon or scheme they can fashion to use against me that will be victorious. You are the light of the world and I choose to shine Your presence upon every situation and upon every battlefield. I choose to be a good soldier that I may fight the good fight of faith. I confess my weakness to fight the enemy and I proclaim my dependency upon You and the weapons that You have given to me that are divinely powerful. I confess that You are worthy to receive all the glory, O God, and not man. I praise You and I thank You that You can tear down every fortress that has been built up in my life.

Day Three

What joy there is in walking from darkness into the marvelous light of God's presence and His Word. There is no greater peace than having come out of a place of bondage and walking through the gates of freedom. No greater satisfaction than journeying through the wastelands of famine and coming into the land of plenty. Far too long have the children of light, God's children, groped about in the darkness, stumbling and losing their way. Too long have we allowed the enemy to trample underfoot the holiness of God and mock His Holy Word. We are fast losing our religious freedom in America. There are those who are endeavoring to remove every remnant of Christianity from our government, public education, the public arena and our society. Consider the following rulings of the U.S. Supreme Court: "secular humanism" declared a religion in 1961; class prayer banned from public schools in 1962; class Bible reading banned from public school facilities in 1963; posting of the Ten Commandments banned in public schools in 1963; and banned teaching of Biblical creationism in public schools in 1987.

If you are like me, every time I read how far we have strayed from God in our country, the first question that comes to mind is, "How did this happen"? Let me take you back to the foundation of our Country for just a moment. America's Declaration of Independence gives us six Christian beliefs: belief in Creator; human beings are created by God; absolute moral laws given by God; governments established by God; belief in the providence of God; and belief in a day of judgment by God. Fifty-two of the 55 signers of this great document were deeply committed Christians. Of the first 108 universities founded in America today, 106 were distinctly Christian. What a contrast to what we have today!

- Christian Index Article 123.

Our founding fathers were wise enough to remove church from state, but not God from state. They understood that allegiance to God was first and foremost, which would cultivate a common wealth of love and respect among its citizens and ensure blessings upon the land. They were right. Let me quote some of these great men that through God's choosing and enabling helped found the land of the free, America.

"All men are created equal, that they are endowed by their Creator with certain unalienable rights, that among them are life, liberty and the pursuit of happiness — that to secure these rights governments are instituted among men, deriving their just powers from the consent of the governed ....." He also wrote: "God who gave us life gave us liberty. Can the liberties of a nation be secure when we have removed a conviction that these liberties are the gift of God?" He also wrote: "Almighty God hath created the mind free. ... All attempts to influence it by temporal punishments or burdens...are a departure from the plan of the Holy Author of our religion..." He also wrote: "I have sworn upon the altar of God eternal hostility against every form of tyranny over the mind of man."

Thomas Jefferson

President George Washington said this when proclaiming our National Thanksgiving Holiday: *"It is the duty of all nations to acknowledge the providence of Almighty God ...."* Later, Abraham Lincoln wrote these words about the Bible: *"In regard to this great book, I have but to say, it is the best gift God has given to men. All the good Savior gave to the world was communicated through this book. But for it we could not know right from wrong."*

Our sense of right and wrong and our sense of wisdom come from the use of reason and common sense, but also and importantly from the Bible, which by faith was considered by our Founding Fathers to be God's inspired text and not just from the mind or heart of man. This faith led to the mottos: "In God We Trust" & "One Nation Under God." Our Founding Fathers were believers in the God of the Bible, even if some were not Orthodox Christians, and they put that faith into the Declaration of Independence, into our laws, into our national monuments, and into our culture.

Abraham Lincoln

The cry from Heaven, I believe, is this; "The foundation has been torn up." The foundation is what sustains the life of what has been built and without it life will perish. Without a solid foundation the building will not stand! We have scorned the Living God in our land by removing the principles of His truth that have made our country so blessed and great. Over 40 million babies have been killed through abortions, one out of every three women will be sexually assaulted, pornography is at an all- time high, half of all marriages end in divorce, adultery is no longer a shameful occurrence, but is swept under the rug and tolerated. We have a government comprised of those who have turned a deaf ear to the God in Heaven; the very One Who has allowed them to hold their places of influence. They are surrounded with reminders upon their sacred buildings and remembrances adorning their great halls that God is the reason this country exists. Yet, they close their eyes to these evidences of faith, thereby breaking down the solid foundation of truth upon which the pillars of a great country were established. Destroy the foundation and the pillars will follow.

This, beloved, has everything to do with Spiritual Warfare and the weapons of the battle. Take your prayer time to seek God's face as you study His Word and then we'll begin. Let's journey back once again to II Corinthians 10:3-5 and read through this mighty passage of Scripture. We saw yesterday that our weapons of warfare are divinely powerful to bring down fortresses. As you read through these verses again, write down the three things that our spiritual weapons can destroy. The first we already know, fill in the remaining two.

Spiritual Weapons Are Divinely Powerful for the Destruction Of

1. Fortresses

2. _____

3. _____

The weapons that God has given to us have the supernatural power to tear down, to destroy *fortresses*, *speculations* and ***every lofty thing raised up against the knowledge of God***. What power, precious one…what power! And as we saw yesterday, it's all to His glory and His magnificent beauty so all the world will worship the One True Living God. These three things destroy our foundations. These we must learn to identify if we are going to protect the foundations God has laid or possibly repair the foundations that have been destroyed already. We looked at fortresses yesterday, beloved, and saw through our Word Study that a fortress can be: *a castle, a stronghold and anything on which one relies. A fortress speaks of arguments and reasoning by which a disputant endeavors to fortify his opinion and defend it against his opponent.* Haven't we seen this take place in our country? If we turn from God to rely on another, we have built a fortress against God that will tear down the foundation. When we allow disputes to arise unchallenged that oppose God's Truth and His way, we have allowed a fortress to rise to power that is an enemy of the foundations God has laid. The fortresses that have been erected in our land are too numerous to count. Look up the following verses and note what you learn about God's foundations and foundations in general.

Psalm 89:14

_____

_____

Isaiah 26:18

_____

_____

Proverbs 10:25

_____

_____

Luke 6: 46-49

_____

_____

Luke 14:28-29

_____

_____

I Corinthians 3:10-11

_____

_____

I Timothy 6:18-21

_____

_____

According to all we have just read how important is the foundation? What foundation should we be laying, supporting, protecting?

_____

_____

_____

This brings us to our blessed Principle of Truth for today, dear student! Read it aloud so you can hear it and let it sink deeply into the recesses of your heart and saturate your mind.

$\mathcal{P}$RINCIPLE

THE FOUNDATIONS OF GOD MUST BE PROTECTED AT ANY COST

Whose responsibility is it to protect the foundations of God that have been laid for us? Explain your answer.

_____

_____

_____

When a foundation is broken up, who do you think is responsible? Explain your reasoning.

_____

_____

God's foundations are necessary for life and if they are destroyed upon the earth, our lives will be sorely affected, and so will the lives of our children and grandchildren. These foundations have crumbled underneath the complacency of the Church and by the pressures of ungodly fortresses. God laid them for us, beloved, but it is our heavenly duty to protect them and rebuild them when necessary. This is why it is absolutely vital that we know our weapons of warfare. Although we are learning what our weapons are for and about their power, we must also learn how to *use* these weapons. It does no good to know what a weapon is for and how powerful it is if we do not know how to use it! Amen? So bear with me, beloved, for we, too, are building a solid foundation of truth for Spiritual Warfare! Foundations take time and they must be fully laid before we begin to build upon them.

In the light of this, let's continue to lay our foundation by looking at the next enemy of God's foundation on our list that our weapons are to destroy. The next one given to us is, *"Speculations."* So we have a clear understanding of what a speculation is, let's locate its meaning in our Word Windows Section. Record your findings in the space provided.

Speculations

_____

_____

Based on your word study, how would you describe the speculations that we are to destroy? How could we recognize these speculations?

_____

_____

We live in a world, an age where speculations arise every day. But, when these speculations arise, what are we to do with them or are we to do anything at all? Are we to turn a deaf ear and ignore them or are we to take a stand against them? How damaging are speculations and how important is it that we take them seriously? Are speculations really a threat? What is my responsibility concerning them? These are questions for which we must have Biblical answers. Turn to the following passages of scripture and note what you learn about speculations from each. Observe what these speculations caused and how they came into existence and what our response to them should be.

Romans 1:20-25

_____

_____

II Timothy 2:23

_____

_____

I Timothy 1: 3-10

_____

_____

_____

How do you think speculations have affected our country and your life?

_____

_____

_____

Based on what we've read in God's Word, how powerful can the influence of speculations that are unbridled and unchallenged be in one's life? Explain your answer.

_____

_____

_____

The third enemy of God's foundations is the *"lofty things"* raised up against the knowledge of God. What do you think a "lofty thing" might be?

_____

_____

It's easy to get the picture in our minds when we hear the word lofty as something that is high, like being up in a loft, right? But, why would a thing that is lofty (high) need to be raised if it is already lifted up? To help steer us in the direction of correct interpretation, let's locate the meaning for *"Lofty"* and *"Raised"* in our Word Windows Section. Write down your findings in the space given.

Lofty

_____

_____

Raised

_____

_____

Based on your findings, what is a *"lofty thing"* that is *"raised up"* against the knowledge of God?

_____

_____

_____

Let's think back to our enemy, the devil. What was he when God created him? What position did he hold? Write out a brief description of him before he sinned against God.

_____

_____

_____

Do you think it's safe to describe him as "lofty"? Explain why or why not.

_____

_____

I believe that Satan, most definitely, fits within the defining boundaries of one who was "lofty", simply because God created him to fill one of the highest angelic positions of Heaven. He had the seal of perfection and his adornment was beyond any beauty that we could imagine upon the earth. He attended to the most holy place in heaven, the altar of God. He was the anointed Cherub, the guardian of the sacred altar before the throne of God. He held a lofty position, beloved, but something happened. Pride was found in his heart and the lust for power gave birth to sin. Though he was high and lofty, he raised himself up against the knowledge of God. This is what he is still doing today, beloved. Now, it is our duty to protect that knowledge with the spiritual weapons of warfare because they are divinely powerful to destroy these lofty things! Let's read our Principle of truth out loud and follow it with our Life Application for today.

Principle: Because the foundations of God must be protected at any cost,

LIFE APPLICATION

I MUST DESTROY EVERY OPPOSITION ON THE SPIRITUAL PLANE

It is our God -given duty to hold trenches of holiness in total faith in Him. He has declared in His Word that we are the destructive forces for the spiritual enemies seeking to break up the foundations of truth and who oppose God's Kingdom. . When the foundations are destroyed, so will the lives that have been built upon them. We must protect, we must re-lay the forgotten foundations and let out a war cry to all the builders of God saying:

ISAIAH 58: 12

"Those from among you will rebuild the ancient ruins; you will raise up the age-old foundations; and you will be called the repairer of the breach, The restorer of the streets in which to dwell."

May you be found re-building the ancient ruins upon the holy foundations! We need the builders to arise, beloved warrior. Will you be counted as one of them? Let's close with our confession of truth for today. Read it aloud and I'll see you on Day Four! I'm so proud of you.

My Confession of Truth

I confess that I am responsible for the conditions of Your foundations, God. I am to repair the breach that has caused a falling away of all that is pure and lovely in Thy sight. I am the defender of Holiness upon the earth and it is my God-given right to destroy every fortress, every speculation and every lofty thing that raises itself up against the knowledge of God. I confess the urgency of the hour for night is coming and I must take up my weapons of warfare and lay the foundation while it is still day.

Day Four

I sat glued to the TV as the interview was taking place between the reporter and a convicted serial killer. It was obvious that the reporter was nervous as she sat down in the chair to begin the interview. The man, who sat before her, had committed the most heinous crimes by torturing his victims and then, eating their flesh over a period of time. She struggled to keep her composure as he gave some of the gory details of his killings. As the interview progressed, it was clear that one dominate theme was emerging from the answers he gave to the reporter as she questioned him. There was a war of evil raging in his mind, a war of life and death. He confessed to hearing voices that prompted him to kill and voices that prompted him to eat of his victim's flesh. He described the subtlety of the attacks on his mind when they began. It started with just a thought about what it would be like to hurt another person. From there, it progressed to fantasizing about killing and then, to the actual taking of a life and eating of the flesh. Although he did not realize what he was doing at the time, he was not only admitting to the crimes, but he was making a confession of truth found in God's word about the power of the mind.

Countless interviews have been conducted with serial killers, murderers, rapists and sexual predators and they all conclude with the same predominate truth; their crimes began in the battlefield of their mind. It began with a thought received from a book, a magazine, a song, a movie, the Internet or even voices of the unknown speaking into their minds. The enemy introduces the idea of sin usually through a thought first. Once he has implanted the seed of that thought, he will begin to water it, feed it and cause it to grow in strength and size, not letting up until it brings forth a destructive fruit. The mind is the doorway through which Satan enters into the lives of people. It's this doorway and the mind itself that we want to focus our attention on today. We will also cover this again later in our study as we immerse ourselves into the armor of God. Pray before you begin your study, beloved, and I'll meet you back here.

Let's start our study time together today by holding up our left hand and saying aloud our five unseen resistances. These five resistances will stay with you for your entire life if you will continue to repeat them over and over again, making them permanent. If you remember, we've been studying in depth a portion of Scripture taken from II Corinthians 10:3-5. Look over these verses and as a way of review, write out the five things about our spiritual weapons that we saw on Day One of our study this week.

1. _____

2. _____

3. _____

4. _____

5. _____

I want us to read through these verses once more and this time focus on the last thing we are told that our weapons of warfare are to do. I've started the sentence for you.

<u>We are taking</u> _____

_____

According to this truth, what are the weapons of warfare taking into bondage and into captivity?

_____

I don't want us to miss this little nugget, beloved, so bear with me. According to this verse, what kind of thoughts do the weapons of our warfare take captive? How many, etc.?

_____

If you answered "every thought", then you are right, beloved! Sometimes, we are so busy trying to tag the bad thoughts that we let down our defenses on the seemingly harmless ones or those thoughts that may not necessarily come in as "bad." There have been many "good" thoughts that have led people, including myself, away from God's will and plan for their lives. This is why our weapons are to take "EVERY thought" captive. So how many thoughts does that leave as free ranging?

_____

ZERO! You are exactly right. Thoughts, good or bad, must be sent through the holy sifter to filter it out or give it a rite of passage to stay. Whatever stays, beloved, will bear fruit at some point in our lives. The mind is the control board of the flesh and the spirit. Let me show you this in Scripture. Look up the following verses and note what you learn about the mind from each. Observe the control, the power and the vulnerability of our mind, etc.

So we have a clear understanding of what a thought is or what is meant by the use of the word *"Thought"* in II Corinthians 10:5, let's turn to our Word Windows Section and locate the definition. Record your findings.

Thought

_____

_____

I Chronicles 28:9

_____

_____

Psalm 16:7

_____

_____

Proverbs 17:20

_____

_____

Isaiah 21:4

_____

_____

Isaiah 26:3

_____

_____

Lamentations 3: 21-24

_____

_____

Matthew 16:23

_____

_____

Romans 7:23

_____

_____

Romans 8:6-7

_____

_____

Ephesians 4: 17-23

_____

_____

In light of the verses you've looked at, why would it be important to take every thought captive?

_____

_____

I want us to see what it means to take every thought captive to the obedience of Jesus Christ by looking at the word meaning for *"Captive."* Turn to your Word Windows Section and locate this definition and record it in the space provided.

Captive

_____

_____

Our thoughts, beloved, are not to be free! This is the challenge of the one who is free in Christ because it seems natural to let our minds run free, unchained and untamed. God gives us weaponry to take up against not only some thoughts, but "ALL THOUGHTS" in order to bring them into captivity. Our thoughts are like wild horses; they will trample, they will run off into dangerous places, they will want no bounds, and in the end they will be found worn out and far away from the place they knew as home. This brings us to our Principle for today, beloved warrior.

℘RINCIPLE

OUR THOUGHTS ARE NOT TO BE GIVEN FREEDOM

We are told over and over again in the word of God that the mind is the control board to the body and the spirit. We must guard it by taking our thoughts captive. Once we have chained those thoughts, where are we to take them from there? Where do the prisoners go? Let's answer this together. Finish the sentence I've started for you based on II Corinthians 10:5

WE ARE TAKING EVERY THOUGHT CAPTIVE TO...

_____

We are to take our prisoners to the school of Jesus by aligning them with His teaching. If a thought cannot be obedient to Jesus Christ, then it must be sent to death row and executed immediately, beloved. Disobedient thoughts must not be allowed to live in the battlefield of our mind. Let us say this once more as a powerful nugget of truth. Read it aloud with me, beloved, because it's too powerful to read over in haste. We need to pause, breathe and take it in. This is a Power Box of Truth for us today!!! I am slapping myself as I type!!!!

Power Box of Truth

> ### DISOBEDIENT THOUGHTS MUST NOT BE ALLOWED TO LIVE IN THE BATTLEFIELD OF OUR MIND.

To slap ourselves a little bit more, let's read the following verses and note how we might put these thoughts to death, or take them captive. We can also learn about the benefits of doing so!

Luke 10:27

_____

_____

Colossians 3:2

_____

_____

I Corinthians 14:20

_____

_____

Hebrews 11:13-15

_____

_____

What a powerhouse of encouragement the saints of old are to us as we read of their lives and of knowing they believed in Jesus without seeing Him just as we have, precious one! They lived by faith, sight unseen and they laid their lives down for their faith without wavering. How? Because they learned to take every obedient thought to Jesus, they learned to take the disobedient ones to death row and not allow them to live in the battlefield of their mind. In doing so, they became the great spiritual giants that we have the blessing to read about today. This brings us to our Life Application today. Read your Principle aloud and follow it with your Life Application Truth.

Principle: *Because our thoughts are not to be given freedom:*

LIFE APPLICATION

I MUST MAKE MY MIND A SLAVE OF JESUS CHRIST

Our mind is to be fully surrendered to the Lord and His Word, or we will lose in the battlefield of our thinking and we will be led away as captives by our own thoughts. We must lay hold of the truth that our weaponry is divinely powerful and able to take captive every thought to the obedience of Jesus Christ. We must make our minds the slaves of the Lord and there, let Him reign in power and beauty. You have been such a diligent student this week and especially today, because I've worked you a little longer! (Ms. Shirley did you hang in there, precious?) I had to mention my precious Ms. Shirley because she is such a trooper when I'm long-winded!! Lots of love to you! I have to pause and take a moment to brag, as any proud mama would, over her children… My Journey Class is the absolute Bomb! They put up with this lowly Bible Teacher and all her wild and crazy things without the first attempt to run away!!! What a class!! I am so proud to be your teacher as no one else would have me! Big hug to all of you. Okay, I'm finished. I just had to burst about my wonderful ladies for a moment that I'm so crazy about and so, so proud of, that I can hardly stand it!

Let's review our week by looking over our Principles and Life Applications and writing them in on our Week in Review boxes. This should be a time of celebration for us as we look at what the Lord has shown to us. We'll start calling this our time to celebrate our week together!! I love that.

OUR WEEK IN REVIEW

Day One

Principle:

Life Application:

Day Two

Principle:

Life Application:

Day Three

Principle:

Life Application:

Day Four

Principle:

Life Application:

I can't emphasize enough the importance of review and repetition. It will stick, beloved, it will stick! Take a quick minute and write out your memory verse including the scripture reference. See if you can write it without looking!

MEMORY VERSE

_____

_____

_____

_____

Let's read aloud our Confession of Truth for today.

My Confession of Truth

Lord, I am a warrior in the arm of the Living God. I am not alone in the battlefield and I am not without my weaponry. You have given to me weapons for the right hand and the left that are of divine power because they are not found in the strength of my flesh. My weapons are from You and with them I can and will take every thought captive to the obedience of Jesus Christ. Every disobedient thought I will slay with the truth of Your Word and I will not allow it to live in the battlefield of my mind. My mind is the slave of Jesus Christ and I will not allow any thoughts to run free, but rather, I will take them as the Lord's prisoner and let Him do with them as He pleases. I confess my mind as the battlefield that the enemy uses to attack every area of my life.

We'll close out our week of study with our Personal Evaluation time. I want to encourage you to take your time with these and not rush them by getting in a hurry to finish. This is a most important step in our Bible Study process as it makes us think through the application of truth into our lives. I love and appreciate you!

Personal Evaluation

What weapons are you using to fight in the spiritual battles of life?

_____

_____

_____

_____

Do you recognize the power of spiritual weapons? If so, how?

_____

_____

_____

_____

Do you have any fortresses erected in your life that you have not destroyed? If so, explain why and what you need to do.

_____

_____

_____

_____

Do you speculate, beloved? Do you accept easily the speculations of others? What should you do in response to speculations?

_____

_____

_____

_____

Are there lofty things that have been raised in your mind, in your life? What are you doing or what do you need to do with these "lofty things"?

_____

_____

_____

_____

What thoughts have you let run free in your mind? What areas of your mind have you not placed the boundaries of God's Word around?

_____

_____

_____

_____

Session Notes

LESSON FIVE

Taking Up Buckler and Shield

The LORD is a Warrior; The LORD is His Name.

Exodus 15:3

Taking Up Buckler and Shield

Day One

It's relatively easy to embrace the thought that God is loving and compassionate and merciful. We find comfort in these truths so our heart gravitates to the realness of them with all the hope that these things are really true for us personally. God designed us to love and to be love because He instilled within us the immeasurable gift of the ability to receive love and to extend it. To secure this understanding for us, God patterned this love for us because I John 4:19 tells us *"We love because He first loved us,"*. Everything that God intends for us to live He first patterns it for us by fleshing it out before our eyes through His provisions, His word, through circumstances, through prayer, and through the life of Jesus, Who became flesh and dwelt among us so we could behold His glory (John 1:14.) It's usually a more comfortable topic of discussion even for non-Christians that God is love. While it is true that God is love, love is only one facet of God's character. God is love but He is Holy, He is fire but He is mercy, He gives and yet, He takes. God is so personal yet, still a mystery.

But what about war? What about taking life even of children and allowing death to take place? Why does God allow these things and does this mean that God isn't a God of love? War is the absence of peace and the presence of conflict. God is a warrior because there is a conflict of good and evil taking place every day, thieving away peace from the world. This war is not contained in battlefields, laden with earth and clay but in the fields of our homes, the lives of our children, the Intensive Care Units, our Nation's Capitol, our neighborhoods, our schools and doctor's offices. It's even taking place within the walls of our churches and other religious organizations. The war- ravaged places are not stained with blood but with tears; tears of those who suffered the loss of great things. There are none who are not susceptible to the damages of Spiritual Warfare for we are all in the battlefields, beloved. In the fields of war every soldier must be trained and equipped so they can withstand and conquer their enemy. This is the reason the Lord has allowed me to write this course of study.

We have seen through the study of God's Word that we are in a Spiritual Warfare . we've seen the enemy we are at war with and why we are at war with him. It does no good to fight if you don't know what you are fighting for! Amen? We now turn our attentions to the weaponry of God. As always, let's bow our knees before the Father, seeking His favor and His wisdom as we open up our hearts and minds to His Word today. Then we'll get started.

Let's begin by reading through what will be your memory verse for this week. This is a powerful verse to memorize for Spiritual Battle, beloved, so I encourage you to set your heart to storing it deep so as not to forget it. Read it aloud several times through.

MEMORY VERSE

Zephaniah 3:17

"The LORD your God is in your midst, A victorious warrior. He will exult over you with joy, He will be quiet in His love, He will rejoice over you with shouts of joy."

Now, I want you to do something that I like to do with scripture that helps personalize it for me. Write out this verse in the space provided but make it personal by adding in your personal pronouns like; my and me. Then read it out loud! We want our enemies in the unseen realm to hear us declare this truth. I've started it for you.

The LORD **MY** God is in _____

_____

_____

Do you not just love this scripture? To know that the LORD, my God is in my midst is an awesome truth and then, to add to that: He is a victorious warrior just removes all fear and anxiety, doesn't it? It's empowering when we personalize scripture; it makes it real to us and our situation. Based on what you have just seen in your memory verse, what does this mean to your life?

_____

_____

_____

_____

_____

Have you ever known God as your warrior? Can you think of a time when God fought for you personally? Write out a brief description. If you cannot think of one, then write out a prayer, asking God to show you the times He has fought for you and maybe you didn't recognize it was His doing. He's so faithful to do that for us if we will but ask Him.

_____

_____

_____

Typed out for you are two verses from Romans chapter 13. Read through them one time and then, write down what truths are found here and what do they mean to you as a child of God?

<u>Romans 13:11-12</u>

11. Do this, knowing the time, that it is already the hour for you to awaken from sleep; for now salvation is nearer to us than when we believed.

12. The night is almost gone, and the day is near. Therefore let us lay aside the deeds of darkness and put on the armor of light.

Take a colored pencil and mark every reference to time such as; hour, day, night and the word, time itself, by drawing a clock around each one. Use the color that you wish and when you are finished, go back and look at these markings. Note what you learn from your markings and then answer the questions that follow.

According to this passage, what time is ending and what time is coming?

_____

_____

There are three things we are told to do in light of the time that is approaching. I don't want us to miss these so I've started each one for you. Finish each sentence according to the verse.

Awaken _____

Lay aside _____

Put on _____

God is merciful to reveal to us that a day is coming when we won't be able to work for Him any longer. He goes on to pour out even more grace by showing us what we must do to be ready for that day. Isn't He wonderful? He tells us to awaken from sleep, lay aside the deeds of darkness, and to put on the armor of light. Let's look at each of these words as we are given them. The first is **"awaken"**. We can't serve God if we're sleeping so this is pretty understandable, isn't it?

Turn to your **Word Windows Section** and retrieve the meaning for this word, *"Awaken."* Record your findings in the space provided.

Awaken

_____

_____

Based on this word study, what do you think it might mean to awaken? What would this imply about a person if they are told to awaken?

_____

_____

Turn to Revelation 3:1-3 in your Bible and read these verses that refer to the Church at Sardis. As you read about this body of believers, note what you see about their condition and what the Lord is warning them to do and why.

_____

_____

_____

Was the Lord pleased with this church? Explain your answer.

_____

_____

To help me remember this church and their state, I call them "Sardine" because the Lord said they were dead. So, instead of Sardis, they are Sardine to me! Their sleeping condition the Lord referred to as dead. When you are dead, beloved, there is no what? _____,

LIFE! We know that obviously the Lord wasn't talking about a physical death so what do you think He means?

_____

_____

Turn to James 2:17-26 and write out how this might apply to what we've just read.

_____

_____

Let's look at a couple of more verses and see what they reveal about this same topic. Record your insights by each one.

Hebrews 6:1

_____

_____

Hebrews 9:14

_____

_____

Based on the things we've just seen in God's Word, can we have a faith that is dead?

_____

_____

We must take into account that the Lord was speaking to the Church, the body of Christ, Christians, in all the accounts we've just read. As a child of God, it is possible for me to have a faith that has died for he tells us that a faith by itself is dead. A faith not in action, beloved, needs to awaken! But on the other hand, faith is the shoes to our works. We don't want dead faith or dead works! We can't be working for the Lord apart from faith and be pleasing to Him. Are there any areas of your faith that lacks works? If so, write these out as a confession before the Lord. Maybe you believe God to take care of your financial needs but yet, you are not tithing as you should; this would be a dead faith. It may be that you believe God forgives but you are still living under the shackles of your past sins; this, too, would be a faith that needs to be revived. Give this some thought and then, write down what the Lord reveals to you.

AREAS OF DEAD FAITH THAT NEED TO BE AWAKENED IN ME

_____

_____

_____

_____

Anyone can quote truth but it takes a faith that is alive to live it. This brings us to our Principle for today.

*P*RINCIPLE

SERVICE IS THE SHOES OF FAITH

I believe that many of us serve the Lord with all the unction and fortitude one can have but we are as bare- footed in faith as we can be. If we were to go back and look over the chart you filled out of dead areas of faith, these would be the areas that need to be "shoed." An area of dead faith is an area that is lacking shoes, beloved. Look over the list you made concerning these areas in your life and write what is needed to bring them to life; what shoes do you need to lace up in these tombs of faith in order to resurrect them? Take time to list these in the space provided for you. Write the dead area first and then the shoe that is needed out beside it. For example, if your tithing was an area of dead faith, then the shoe would be: begin to tithe on a regular basis, beginning with my next pay check or confess that my money is the Lord's, not mine. Sometimes, a good old fashion confession is the shoe we need most! Give this some thought and take your time.

Dead Area	**Shoe Needed (action needed)**

Genuine faith will never be content to lie dormant; it must take action and clothe itself in the raiment of the flesh. Faith is not the garnishment of our service, it is the fuel of our service. Read through your Principle and follow with our Life Application for today.

Because Service is the shoes of Faith then…

LIFE APPLICATION

OUR SERVICE BECOMES THE DECLARATION OF OUR FAITH

What a testimony we have through our service because it declares our belief. Service will follow a faith that is alive. There is such rationale when our flesh doesn't want to serve the Lord in the capacity He has called us to. We reason away our service through excuses like; "I don't really have the time, I have no gifts or talents to offer, I am not like so and so or I don't know enough!" The list goes on and on with the pen of the flesh in hand. It is a true statement; people would rather see a sermon than hear one. What better way to bring your sermon of faith to life than serving so everyone can see it? This is God's plan for all of us who have professed Jesus as Lord!

Let's call it a day and I'll see you tomorrow!

Day Two

Before I surrendered my life to Jesus, I made every attempt to dodge the Lord's advances toward me. I believed in God and His Son, Jesus Christ, but I did not surrender my life unto His Lordship until I was seventeen years of age about to graduate high school. There were so many reasons I had not to give my life to the Lord; the main being the boy I was dating. I was comfortable with my life and the circle of worldly friends I had made. I could do whatever I wanted and I usually did. I didn't have to think about the future or my past; only live for the moment, having fun and enjoying worldly pleasures. I genuinely believed I was happy and that my life would be just like the ones in a fairy tale book; I would get the prince and live happily ever after. Sometimes our dreams and even our self-indulging theology will become the very things that keep us from the life God intends for us to have. It wasn't until I became so miserable with the consequences of my sinful choices that I realized, I was the enemy of my own soul. It wasn't the others, the world or even the devil, it was me. God poured out His waves of conviction and began drawing me with a force that was so undeniable that it could not be hidden physically. Tears became my pillow, agony of soul my bed, and fear of separation from God the anthem of my soul. Finally, when I could bear it no longer, I ran to Him, and collapsing before the throne of grace, I surrendered. I laid down all of me, dreams, desires, my sin, my anger, the hurts of my life, and the harnesses of my will, I handed over to His reign.

How marvelous is the captivating beauty of God's love for us; His unreachable, magnificent presence that pursues each and every one of us as if we were the only soul upon the face of the earth. What marvel of His flight from Heaven soaring across the sinful lands that He may sweep in upon the prey of His heart. The vastness of His love is scandalous, yet, altogether pure and undefiled. What prompts such love? What moves the Holy One from His lofty place to dwell among the lowly? How could this be, beloved? God's grace is too radical for definition and when He sets His affections upon another, there are no boundaries, no qualifications, and no conditions except one; surrender into the hands of love extended. So much of our Christian walk and ability to trust in God is traced back to the threshing floor of grace. It's this threshing floor that will be our goal of study today and our conclusion; total surrender! O precious one, please pray, pray, pray before you begin today and then, pour yourself into this time with the One Who has loved you with such a relentless love that He will never give up on you. Let's pursue Jesus and totally surrender unto Him as we take His hand and walk through the pages of His Word together, today.

Look back at Day One of our study this week and read through Romans 13:11-12 to refresh our minds. Once you've looked over these verses, write out verse 12 in the space provided for you. This will be the verse we will hone in on in our time together today.

Romans 13:12

_____

_____

What is the tone of this verse? Is it giving us praise, a warning, a charge, etc.? Explain your answer.

_____

_____

_____

What are we told to lay aside?

_____

Turn to your Word Windows Section and find the meaning of the phrase, *"Lay Aside"* and record it in the space given to you.

Lay Aside

_____

_____

According to this verse, what is almost gone?

_____

When do people normally sleep, in the day or in the night?

_____

What do you think it means that the night is almost gone?

_____

_____

What is at hand?

_____

We've just been given the reasons that we are to "lay aside" the deeds of darkness. In the following verse of this passage, Romans 13:13, we are given a list of deeds that would be of the darkness. Read this verse and write these things out.

Deeds of Darkness

_____

_____

_____

_____

Based on your word study and the other things we've seen so far, what do you think it might mean to lay aside these things?

_____

_____

_____

Out of these things, which ones, if any, might we see or can we see in the body of Christ? In the walls of the church?

_____

_____

The time for sleeping, for resting, and for pleasure are almost over and the return of the Lord is near. I believe these words written through the hand of Paul are right on target for our day. I believe we are living in the days of darkness; an age where evil deeds are the attire of many and there is no shame before their eyes. But, I believe with absolute certainty of soul, that the sun is just over the horizon and it's rising faster than we realize. When the sun comes up, it exposes what's been done under the cover of darkness. This warning, this earnestness of soul, is a wakeup call; a call to order, a call for repentance and urgency to recognize that the sun is coming up! He calls for a laying down of those deeds that are not godly in order to put on the armor of light. We can't put on until we have put off!

What do you think it would take for a person to lay aside deeds of darkness they have in their life?

_____

_____

What would it take for you, beloved?

_____

_____

Many of us today are engaging in the unseen of Spiritual Warfare, not having taken up the armor of light. We cannot take up the armor of light because we haven't laid aside those deeds done in the darkness. There are two kinds of armor, beloved. There are those of light and those of darkness. Our challenge question is this: what armor are you hiding behind? Are we hiding behind the armor of light or the armor of darkness? This brings us to our Principle for today.

*P*RINCIPLE

ARMOR PROFESSES OUR ALLEGIANCE

The armor of a warrior is the shield of his life. It's what stands between him and his enemy's ammunition. A warrior's armor can mean the difference between life and death out on the battlefield. The armor of a warrior would bear the markings of the king they were fighting for or fighting to defend. The armor itself drew the battle line and declared war just by what it represented. Herein lies a power-packed truth: What your armor represents will determine your enemy. In other words, beloved, if you have the armor of darkness, you are declaring war on the King Who is of the light. But, if you are bearing the armor of Light, you are raising the flag of war, renouncing the kingdom of darkness.

An armor bearer had one sole responsibility: to follow the one he was devoted to into battle, bearing his armor. There was an undying allegiance in battle for the beloved armor bearer. The warrior depended on no flesh in battle except this one lone soul. He carried the weaponry for the valiant one and made his stance sure and steady, side by side with his master. Fleeing in the face of death was not an option and fear did not dictate his heart. I want us to see the beauty and devotion found in the heart of the armor bearer. Read the following verses found in I Samuel 14:1-15 and take in the story that is being told. When you've completed reading, go back through this stretch of scripture once more, only this time mark every reference to the armor bearer, including all pronouns for him or other adjectives such as; "young man", etc. Mark these references by drawing a shield around each one with the color of your choosing. Make a list of what you see regarding the armor bearer.

I Samuel 14:1-15

1. Now the day came that Jonathan, the son of Saul, said to the young man who was carrying his armor, "Come and let us cross over to the Philistines' garrison that is on the other side." But he did not tell his father.

2. Saul was staying in the outskirts of Gibeah under the pomegranate tree which is in Migron. And the people who were with him were about six hundred men,

3. and Ahijah, the son of Ahitub, Ichabod's brother, the son of Phinehas, the son of Eli, the priest of the LORD at Shiloh, was wearing an ephod. And the people did not know that Jonathan had gone.

4. Between the passes by which Jonathan sought to cross over to the Philistines' garrison, there was a sharp crag on the one side and a sharp crag on the other side, and the name of the one was Bozez, and the name of the other Seneh.

5. The one crag rose on the north opposite Michmash, and the other on the south opposite Geba.

6. Then Jonathan said to the young man who was carrying his armor, "Come and let us cross over to the garrison of these uncircumcised; perhaps the LORD will work for us, for the LORD is not restrained to save by many or by few."

7. His armor bearer said to him, "Do all that is in your heart; turn yourself, and here I am with you according to your desire."

8. Then Jonathan said, "Behold, we will cross over to the men and reveal ourselves to them.

9. "If they say to us, 'Wait until we come to you'; then we will stand in our place and not go up to them.

10. "But if they say, 'Come up to us,' then we will go up, for the LORD has given them into our hands; and this shall be the sign to us."

11. When both of them revealed themselves to the garrison of the Philistines, the Philistines said, "Behold, Hebrews are coming out of the holes where they have hidden themselves."

12. So the men of the garrison hailed Jonathan and his armor bearer and said, "Come up to us and we will tell you something." And Jonathan said to his armor bearer, "Come up after me, for the LORD has given them into the hands of Israel."

13. Then Jonathan climbed up on his hands and feet, with his armor bearer behind him; and they fell before Jonathan, and his armor bearer put some to death after him.

14. That first slaughter which Jonathan and his armor bearer made was about twenty men within about half a furrow in an acre of land.

15. And there was a trembling in the camp, in the field, and among all the people. Even the garrison and the raiders trembled, and the earth quaked so that it became a great trembling.

Armor Bearer

_____

_____

_____

_____

_____

_____

_____

Turn to your Word Windows Section located in the back of your study and find the meaning for the words, *"Armor"* and *"Bearer".* Record your findings in the space provided.

Armor

_____

_____

Bearer

_____

_____

Based on what you've seen, how would you describe an armor bearer?

_____

_____

Read the following verses and notice the relationship between the warrior and his armor bearer.

I Samuel 16:21

_____

_____

I Samuel 31:4-6

_____

_____

According to Ephesians 6:11-13, whose armor are we to take up and put on?

_____

O, beloved student, do you see the light of a most precious truth peering through to us? Let me ask you a question to help stir your thinking: Based on what we've just read in Ephesians, who is the armor bearer of God?

_____

_____

In light of what an armor bearer is, what should our relationship be with Him as His armor bearers?

_____

_____

God is the warrior, beloved one, and we are at war with Him, but not as a sole warrior standing in the fields of battle alone, but with Him, bearing His armor. He never sends us into battle alone; He goes before us putting Himself between us and the enemy. Our duty is to take up His armor, His full armor and march into battle behind Him, following only where He leads. Read through our Principle for today and follow it with the Life Application.

Principle: Because Armor professes our allegiance then…

LIFE APPLICATION

THOSE WHO BELONG TO GOD MUST TAKE UP HIS ARMOR

The calling of the armor bearer into the front line of battle, following behind the One He serves, even if it means death. God has given us the right to bear arms in Spiritual Battle. We are to take up all that He has completed, prepared and made, and march through the darkness, bearing the armor of His Light. So, precious armor bearer, valiant warrior in the army of the Living God, stand tall, fully armed, bearing the weaponry of your King. And there among the ancient ruins destroyed by God's enemy long ago, stand and reclaim what He has made, knowing you are His provision to complete the work of the Kingdom of Heaven.

Review your memory verse and then, let's close out our time together by holding up our left hand and calling out our five unseen resistances. I'll see you on Day Three!

Day Three

One of my favorite stories tucked away in the vastness of God's Word is that of David and Jonathan. It's a story of allegiance and uniting of soul between two mighty men of God. David became like a son to Jonathan's father, King Saul. He even became Saul's armor bearer as we saw in our study time on Day Two. Jonathan and David's bond would transcend the love of family and duty. It was undeniable knitting by the hand of God intertwining two souls so tightly that the heart of one was not complete apart from the other. They were two souls dwelling in one together within the chambers of one heart. They vowed their lives to one another and their service no matter the cost. Jonathan, a valiant warrior himself, stripped himself of his armor and extended it to David. In this beats the heart of the armor bearer; to hold, to carry, to give, to love, to live and even to die. This is what an armor bearer does, beloved. They strip off what they have been given in order to give it for the one they love and serve; the one their souls are one with.

This is a choosing that only a powerful, lovingly omnipotent God can orchestrate. This spectacular knitting of His soul to another is beyond comprehension for our simple minds of clay to grasp and take in. It strikes at the deepest portal of the soul and shuts every crevice of our meager and imperfect understanding. It's a reality that fills us up to our emotional brink allowing us to connect with the One Who chose to connect to us. You and I have a multi-faceted bond with the creator God, but at the summit of this relationship is our assignment as armor bearer. God has placed His confidence in us by entrusting us with His power, gifts and weaponry. He chose us to follow Him into battle where all that is dearest to His heart is at stake. What an honor to be enlisted, to be chosen for such a heavenly duty. We want to continue our journey unto the battlefields of the Lord and there, shoulder to shoulder with the Holy One, discover our destiny. Pray, beloved one, and seek the heart of your God asking for understanding and an outpouring of conviction upon your soul.

Today, we begin our plummet into our battle cry, Ephesians 6:10-18. I've typed this out for you and it is at the back of your book rather than here in the lesson, because we'll be using it throughout the remainder of our Woman of War Study. Read through this passage once as a refresher. These verses should be a familiar song to your soul if you've been reading them through every morning and evening. How I pray they are! After you've read through this passage once, write down your thoughts concerning the truths about our role and the charge given to God's children.

My Thoughts

_____

_____

_____

Now let's go back through this power- packed passage of God's Word and this time draw a circle around every reference to the child of God; to the one who is being charged with these truths. These will be the pronouns such as, you and your. Use whatever color you wish, beloved; only take your time to ensure you've marked every reference. Make a list of what you saw based on your markings.

The Warrior

_____
_____
_____
_____
_____

Write out verse 10 word for word. I've started it for you.

Finally _____

_____

What is the child of God commanded to do? What charge is given?

_____

_____

Look up the word meaning for ***"Strong"*** and record it in the space given to you.

Strong

_____

_____

_____

Based on your word study, what do you think it means to be strong in the Lord?

_____

_____

Who are we to be strong in?

_____

Who are we not to be strong in, beloved? Think with me for a moment? If we are not strong in the Lord, who might we try to be strong in?

_____

_____

Has God ever told us to be strong in ourselves? Why do you think this is, explain your answer?

_____

_____

I cannot number the failures and times I have tried to be strong in my own self by placing my confidence in those things I felt secure in or strong. I have planned out my own way of escape, my own plans to accomplish a certain task or bring to completion a goal I had set, only to be miserably disappointed, not to mention hopelessly discouraged. This is where we are in danger of throwing in the towel and throwing our hands up in the air to surrender. Every time we strive in our own strength to fight the battles of life, we are not only fighting with weapons of the flesh but we are doomed to failure before we ever begin. Satan is the master disguiser of false security by raising the platform of self-performance in our own eyes. He yells from the sidelines of life as a doting spectator; "You can do it!" His advice for any who will listen will always be to depend on self above all else. If that won't work, he'll introduce another arm of the flesh as a subtle dependency at first until we are addicted to the support and ability of others.

It's our nature to survive, so as a fleshly reaction, we raise our life support beams under those things that we are strong in, our areas of strength. What do you consider your strengths? Give this question some thought and then, make a list of the strengths that came to mind.

MY STRENGTHS

_____

_____

_____

_____

_____

_____

_____

_____

Do you believe God is strong? If so, what are the strengths of the Lord? How do you think God is strong?

_____

_____

_____

_____

Look up the following verses and write down what you learn about the strength of God.

Deuteronomy 3:24

_____

_____

Deuteronomy 31:6

_____

II Chronicles 25:8

_____

_____

II Chronicles 32:7

_____

_____

Job 9:19

_____

_____

Psalm 24:8

_____

_____

Psalm 35:10

_____

_____

This truth we must make declaration to over and over again, repeating it until our hearts beat as one with the reality that God is strong and there is none who can contend with Him. His hand holds all power and His arms boundless might. This brings us to our Principle for today.

*P*RINCIPLE

IN GOD IS MY SOURCE OF STRENGTH

Before we can deem God as the source of our strength, we must declare our flesh as the source of our weakness. For too long, we have battled in the trenches with fleshly weapons of skill, ability, physical strength, independency, stubbornness, rebelliousness, pride, knowledge, ownership and money among many other things. These false securities latch on to our pride and bridle our dependency upon God with the lie that we can make it on our own. The truth is, beloved, we cannot make it on our own but we can make it with God! With God there are no failures, no losers, no hopeless soul and no insecure heart. SLAP! SLAP! SLAP! Amen and Hallelujah!

We are weak, we are without strength and we are doomed to fail if left to ourselves. God would not hear of His child being in this world without a source of strength, without the safety of His presence. Will you make this confession with me, beloved, by writing out a confession of truth regarding who you are apart from God; the weakness of your flesh? Its absolute freedom at its highest when we acknowledge our inabilities. Confession of independency is the first step to dependency upon God, beloved. Write your bold confession out and read it aloud.

MY CONFESSION OF WEAKNESS

_____

_____

_____

Will you read your Principle aloud and then follow it through with our Life Application for today?

Principle: If God is my source of strength then…

LIFE APPLICATION

MY WEAKNESS IS NO LONGER A HINDRANCE FOR ME

Only God can take our frailties and bind them with cords of His strength and the fortitude of Heaven. He created us with limitations so we would cling to Him. In His unfailing love for you and for me, He declared us "unable" so we could come to know that He is able. So, beloved ARMOR BEARER, I say to you:

BE STRONG IN THE LORD AND IN THE STRENGTH OF HIS MIGHT.

What a trooper you are, I am a proud mama writer right now! I am thanking God for you.

Day Four

Do you have a defining moment in your life where you just knew with all certainty that your life would be forever changed? The story of our life is ever developing and most definitely the road markers of change stand prominent as a reminding declaration of the turns and twists that have revolutionized our journey. I have them, you have them, and we all have them, beloved. Some, we are proud of, while others we wish so badly to erase from our memories. Whatever turns have brought you to the place you are in now, there has been One Who has never left His post of watch care over you. He, with perfect faithfulness, has been at the helm of your life as a steady captain to make certain you make it to the port of His destination. Even though we are battered and storm tossed and our sails torn by the decisions we have made or by the beatings we have endured by the ships of others, our Captain has never left the helm.

As time passes, we awaken more to those things that have left their mark upon our lives. Some marks penetrate deeper than others. Some seem to strike so purposeful, so forceful that we are broken at the core of our being. We have an enemy who strikes with murderous intent to drive us right into the jaws of destruction. Every one of us is susceptible to his ploys and defenseless to stand against the schemes of destruction he seeks to deploy when we standalone. But, how are we to stand against the arsenal he uses? How are we to press on through the maze of our failures, our hurts, and our destructive behaviors? There is good news, beloved! We'll begin to unveil the layers of victory in our last day of study. If you haven't already, pray before you begin!

Let's hold up our left hand and declare our five unseen resistances! When you are finished, record them on the chart provided as way of reminder and solidity.

Five Unseen Resistances

1. _____
2. _____
3. _____
4. _____
5. _____

Oh, the blessed power of repetition! Let's look back at our text of study found in Ephesians 6:10-18. Go back through these verses and mark every reference to the phrase **"stand firm"** by drawing a red circle around each one. Once you are finished, write out what you learned about standing firm. What is our role, what are we to stand firm against and how are we to stand firm?

Stand Firm

_____
_____
_____
_____
_____

Look up the meaning for this phrase "***Stand Firm***" in your Word Windows Section and record your findings.

Stand Firm

_____
_____

Based on this word meaning, what does it mean to stand firm?

_____
_____

Read through these verses once more, but this time mark every reference to weaponry that is given by drawing a line underneath each one using the color of your choice. Once you are finished, list these weapons, this "full armor" of God on the chart provided for you.

Weapons/ The Full Armor of God

_____
_____
_____
_____

God tells us to be strong in Him, but He doesn't stop there. He continues by instructing us how to do that! What does He tell us to do, beloved? How are we strong in Him and in the strength of His might?

_____

_____

_____

Our strength comes from the Lord but it comes through the armor He has extended for His children to take up and put on. This armor is from the Mighty Warrior Himself; it has been tried and tested in many a battle, beginning with the first when Satan fled from Heaven with a third of the angelic hosts. His armor is sure, it is impenetrable and, with it, might and power are a stay for every soul in battle. I want to show this power hidden within these verses. Take a highlighter and highlight every time you see the phrase *"will be able to"*. Once you have found these, write what we will be able to do with this most powerful armor. There are three of them, beloved, and one of them we've already looked at!

I WILL BE ABLE TO

1. _____

2. _____

3. _____

Turn to your Word Windows Section and locate the word meaning for *"Able"* and record your insights in the space provided.

Able

_____

_____

We've looked at the meaning for the phrase *"stand firm"* already in our study, but I want us to look at these two other abilities the armor of God provides for us. Locate them in your Word Windows Section and record your findings beside the corresponding word.

Resist

_____

_____

_____

Extinguish

_____

_____

Based on your word study, what does it mean to be able? What does it mean for you to be able to stand firm, to resist, and extinguish?

_____

_____

_____

What are we able to resist?

_____

What are we able to extinguish?

_____

When you hear the phrase, "flaming arrows" or "fiery darts", what comes to your mind? What is the potential of this kind of ammunition in war?

_____

_____

Flaming arrows or fiery darts are aimed at a selected target so these would be purposeful blows that the enemy would direct to our lives and the fire would be for destruction once it has hit. Fire strikes quickly and catches us off guard and it can engulf its targets in a matter of moments. The dryer the area, beloved, the quicker it burns. I pray that we will not be a fuel for the fire; that we would not be parched ground for the target of the enemy! We must not allow the desert places to remain because these are the bull's eyes for Satan to aim his fiery darts. Fire feeds off of the dry and dead places. Over and over again we see our responsibility to maintain our lives in such a way that we are continually bearing fruit in every good work.

Failure is the absence of ability to succeed. We, as God's children, have been enabled for victory, for success in battle, by the armory God has created for us. But, the secret to this victory lies in the two words, *"will be"*, which implies the resource to be able is there but there is an act on our part that must take place. This brings us to our

$\mathcal{P}$RINCIPLE

I AM ENABLED FOR VICTORY THROUGH THE ARMOR OF GOD

Armor is everything for the one going in to battle. Apart from it, we are exposed and vulnerable to the enemy's strikes. Death is imminent for the one who is unarmed! We can die a slow spiritual death over time or quickly by one strategic blow simply because we have no armor of protection. Our armor is our defense, beloved, and without it we cannot stand; We are not able to withstand the mortar fire coming from the gates of hell sent out to set our life ablaze with destruction. There are two things we are told to do with God's armor. Can you find what they are? I've mentioned them before but see if you can find them. These two things will reveal to us our responsibility in warfare. HINT: They are described with two words each.

_____ _____

_____ _____

If you answered, "take up" or "put on". you answered correctly. How would you describe the difference between taking up something and putting on something? Or, do you believe there is a difference? Explain your answer.

_____

_____

_____

It would do no good for a soldier to march out into the frontlines of battle carrying his armor or have it boxed up neatly in a travel bag! The warrior has a duty to protect himself so he can live to serve another day. Our duties of war are seen in these two acts. We must first take up the armor of God and secondly we must put it on. It's not enough, precious one, to take it up by confessing the need for it or through acknowledging its existence in prayer, we must also put it on. There is a powerful difference between taking up and putting on. This is what we will be learning through our remaining weeks together. In the mean time let's allow this truth to settle in allowing us to savor in the potential fruit harvested in our lives.

Let's take in our principle once again. *We are enabled for victory through the armor of God therefore our ...*

Life Application

ARMOR MUST BE TAKEN UP AND PUT ON

A confession of the armor is a form of taking it up merely through the acknowledgment of its existence and power. We, as God's women, must actively clothe our outward garments with the vital protection that comes with their adornment. No one can put them on you, beloved, this is your duty and yours alone. As much as I can and do pray for my daughters, they must take action to take up the armor of God and then step into it as His child. This truth has taken me many years of defeat to learn. Reflect on this and allow your spirit to receive it in full so your heart and mind can appropriate it in your life. So often we battle the same war over and over again because we are unarmed. What kind of woman are you today? Are you armed or unarmed?

_____

How can this truth affect your walk in the Lord? What are your thoughts concerning the things we have learned today? What do you think your response needs to be?

_____

_____

_____

You cannot put a price on the simplicity of truth given from God's Word. There is no need to enlarge it; it's big enough on its own. There is no need to fluff it or repackage it because it is not for sale! The word of God is pure, infallible and it stands alone as living water for the soul of every thirsty life. I don't know where you are in your walk with the Lord. Maybe you have been beaten and battered for so long you've come to accept this as just the way it's supposed to be; but it isn't. You may be like so many of us, who have become comfortable in the clothing of loss, the garments of failure, that you are afraid to put on something new. But we must, precious armor bearer, we must. There are lives at stake other than our own and with every passing hour the death toll rises, the wounded are suffering, and the missing- in- action continues to climb in number. Night is coming, beloved one, and we must take our stand with Paul and "fight the good fight of faith", fully armed with the weaponry of God.

Write out our memory verse for this week to ensure you have it memorized.

MEMORY VERSE

_____

_____

_____

_____

Let's make our confession of truth for this week.

My Confession of Truth

I am the armor bearer of the Lord and I by Him; take my stand knowing that His armor proclaims victory to my enemies. I confess my need to bear arms and follow the Mighty One into battle. I confess that victory is sure and my armor tested and found more than able. I confess that I am able to stand firm against every scheme of the devil. I am able to resist Him in the evil day and I am able to extinguish every fiery arrow he deploys toward my life. I will be a faithful armor bearer for the Lord and I will praise Him upon the battlefields.

Let's look back over all the wonderful truths the Lord has shown us this week by writing them down in our week in review chart.

OUR WEEK IN REVIEW

Day One

Principle:
Life Application:

Day Two

Principle:
Life Application:

Day Three

Principle:
Life Application:

Day Four

Principle:
Life Application:

God has truly blessed us with the richness of His Word and I give Him all the praise and glory for the faithfulness He displays each and every week for those who seek to know Him more. I am honored to learn and become the mighty woman of war God has created us to be and provided for us to become. Thank you is not adequate to express my heart's gratitude for each and every one of you. I exalt you in the Lord to press on and finish this course with me! Hang in there, precious one. Let's close out our week together through answering our Personal Evaluation Questions. These are always so painful for me, precious student. Please know that before these truths hit you, God has beaten me with them already! I've said many times over, long before my studies hit the hands of women, they have slapped the fire out of me! Just know this my sweet friend and fellow comrade, my soul dances over you at the writing of this study! For all the blessings to come in your life, for all the victories fixed upon your horizons, and for every enemy of God you will slay upon the battlefields of truth; I dance over you!

Love you so much!

Personal Evaluation

Do you know your role in battle? If so explain.

_____

_____

_____

_____

What are you to be for God out in the battlefields, beloved? How are you fulfilling this in your life now; if not, what do you need to do?

_____

_____

_____

_____

Do you live enabled or disabled in spiritual warfare? Explain how or why?

_____

_____

_____

_____

What weapons are you fighting with? What strengths are you depending on?

_____

_____

_____

_____

What do you need to do in light of all that you have learned this week?

_____

_____

_____

_____

_____

What are you to do with the armor God has given you? What have you not done with it thus far?

_____

_____

_____

_____

_____

_____

Are there battles you continue to lose over and over again? If so, why do you think this is? What do you need to change or appropriate that you haven't?

_____

_____

_____

_____

_____

Session Notes

LESSON SIX

Dressed For War

Dressed For War

"Line up the shield and buckler, and draw near for the battle!"

Jeremiah 46:3

Day One

"Dress for success" is a phrase often heard in the corporate world which reflects the ideology that our attire is a contributing factor to achievement. This philosophy, although true on many levels, can paralyze us with fear, especially if we lack self-confidence or struggle with insecurities about our looks. Because of the nature and weakness of the flesh, our attire can enhance emotions in such a way that we can feel more empowered, accepted, attractive, confident and even happy. Strange as it may sound, many times our outward appearance can end up being our own worst critic. There have been countless casualties of the confidence battle with just one glance in the mirror! How we view ourselves on the outside can ravish all, if any, assurance we may have if we fear disapproval. Society is most certainly site motivated with the mentality if someone looks like they have it all together, they probably do.

Our value as a woman is assaulted daily by the bombardment of magazines splashing across the front-page the epitome of fashion and body size. We can't even shop for groceries without a self-esteem confrontation. We're slapped in the face with it every time we enter the shopping arena, not to mention the mannequins are usually sporting a size zero. Who wears a size zero? Really? The Hollywood scene is surrounded by such hype with any event taking place and the focus is usually on what the women are wearing! Who designed whose gown and there's the infamous day-after critiquing of the best and worst dressed of the evening! It's like putting yourself in an open field for the wolves to ravage; and ravage they do. How pleased our adversary is when we make prey of our own flesh.

Our world is so indoctrinated with the importance of outward appearances that inner beauty has been forced into the shadows of insignificance. Self-esteem is planted in vain in the rocky soil of approval from others; it will only yield a harvest of disappointment. Sad to say, most opinions are formed at first sight. We want people who are "easy on the eyes", don't we? Being sight driven can lead us blindly to empty places. So, what's the answer? The spiritual reality is this, dear student; it is our character that we should dress every day. If you're dressing your character every morning, there won't be a problem with your outward appearance. This is vitally true in Spiritual Warfare. If we dress the inwardness of our being, our outward existence will follow accordingly. Our path of study this week will be dressing for success in battle. If you haven't already sought the Lord's blessing through prayer, then take time to do so.

Read through Ephesians 6:10-18 as way of review. Hold up your left hand and call out your five unseen resistances. How I pray that God will take His finger and etch them with holy fire upon the frontals of your mind.

Read through these verses once more (remember they are typed out for you in the back of your study book) and note how much of the armor we are to put on.

_____

_____

God gives clear instruction to His combat children to take up and to put on the FULL armor of God. Based upon this truth, where does our armor come from? Where can it be found?

_____

_____

Do you think God is speaking of a literal suit of armor? Explain.

_____

_____

Turn to your Word Windows Section and find the meaning for the word, *"Full"* and record your findings in the appropriate space given.

Full

_____

_____

Based on the truth you have gleaned from the meaning of this word, what do you think this means for you? How should we adjust our lives, if any?

_____

_____

_____

_____

How important would it be for a solidier going out to battle to have his full armor?

_____

_____

Incomplete armor means incomplete protection, leaving a soldier unequipped to stand in the day of battle. When we fail to dress appropriately, we fail to do battle effectively. God gives us life training in these verses in Ephesians instructing each of us to suit up for battle and to suit up completely. God is not speaking of a literal armor to clothe our physical bodies with, He is describing a spiritual armor. Remember, beloved, what kind of war we are in? What is our "struggle" against? Who and what are we waging war with?

_____

_____

_____

Is our battle, our warfare, against flesh and blood?

_____

Since our battle is not against flesh and blood, then our armor is not a physical armor. We battle on the spiritual plain against the unseen world; therefore, our weapons are unseen as well. They are spiritual weapons that arm our spirit. Our weaponry falls into two categories: **Offensive** and **Defensive**. Go through our warfare verses in Ephesians 6 once more but this time circle every piece of armor that is given. Take into account that our armor is that which protects us, that which we wear. Armor is our defensive weaponry. There are five things given to us that cover the soldier of God with protection. Write these out in the spaces given.

1. _____

2. _____

3. _____

4. _____

5. _____

The full armor of God includes girding our loins with truth (the belt of truth), the breastplate of righteousness, shod our feet with the preparation of the Gospel of peace (the shoes of peace), the shield of faith, and the helmet of salvation. I want to encourage you to recite them this way: Read these aloud three or four times helping to seal them in our hearts. Knowing all the pieces is vital to powerful, victorious living. Don't worry about their meaning just yet, we are getting to that. For now, just begin learning them and committing them to memory.

BELT OF TRUTH

BREASTPLATE OF RIGHTEOUSNESS

SHOES OF PEACE

SHIELD OF FAITH

HELMET OF SALVATION

As you read through these pieces of armor, write out beside each one which part of the body this piece of armor might be protecting for a soldier in battle.

Piece of Armor   Area of Protection

Belt of Truth   ⟹   _____

Breastplate of Righteousness   ⟹   _____

Shoes of Peace   ⟹   _____

Shield of Faith   ⟹   _____

Helmet of Salvation   ⟹   _____

These powerful five pieces of our armor we will call out on our right hand just like we did with our five unseen resistances on our left. Psalm 45:4 tells us; *"And in Your majesty ride on victoriously, for the cause of truth and meekness and righteousness; let Your right hand teach You awesome things."* The right hand is the symbol of authority and power. This is the reason we will learn them on this hand, the ordained hand of strength and victory. These give every child of God authority to do battle and power to be victorious in battle. Take your pen or pencil and write these five unseen armor pieces on your palm chart of the right hand.

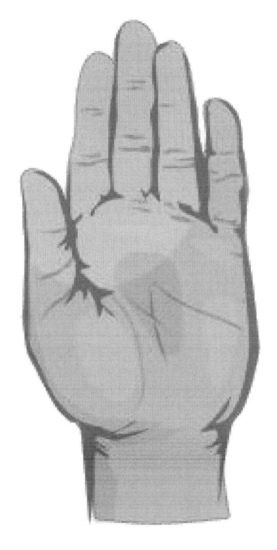

These five pieces are easy to remember by noticing that: it's the Two **B's,** Two **S's** and an **H**! Say these five unseen armor pieces again aloud as you hold up each finger one at a time. This is your hand of power! These five are your defenses against those five unseen resistances we recite on our left hand. God has given us five pieces of armor because there are five unseen resistances that wage war against us. It does no good to study our enemy if we don't put that knowledge into action by knowing our defenses to *"stand firm"* against them. We can stand firmly against every war waged, every battle declared against our lives and our very soul. Without these, we will not be able to stand. Let's take each of these one at a time beginning with the Belt of Truth. Let me begin by asking you a question: barring fashion, what purpose does a belt usually serve when someone puts it on?

_____

_____

A belt holds up everything else, doesn't it? It's a necessary piece of clothing vital to holding the other garment pieces in place. Without the belt, you are in danger of losing vital pieces of covering! This was a very important piece to the Roman soldier's armor. The Roman soldier put around his waist a very wide belt which, not only held the rest of his pieces in place, but it was also the holder for a lot of equipment. There was a loop, for example, for the different swords. Other loops held ropes and a rations sack. When the legions conquered a city, the soldiers would empty out the ration sack to make room for gold, jewelry, and other loot they picked up. There were loops on the belt for darts. The belt was tied in several places to stay in place, so that no matter how the soldier moved about, fell down, climbed hills, etc., the belt was always in place with weapons at the ready. If the belt were not on straight, then everything would be out of place for the soldier. This would cut down his efficiency in battle and may even cost him his life.

It's the understanding of this basic, simple truth that God wants us to understand. He wants us to get it. It's why He begins with this piece of armor and not the others. This piece is what every other piece depends on to be held secure and kept in its proper place. Truth is like the watchdog for all the other pieces! Look up the Word meaning for *"Truth"* and record it in the space.

Truth

_____

_____

_____

Why do you think truth would be so vital?

_____

_____

With this in mind, what is not found in our adversary, the devil? We learned this in one of our previous weeks of study. If you need help remembering, look at John 8:44 in your Bible.

_____

_____

_____

Truth is what separates good from evil, right from wrong, sin from righteousness and light from darkness. It's the divide secured and held by the hand of a holy God declaring throughout the ages that His truth will prevail for all eternity. The belt of truth, beloved, is the divide that secures us. Truth has been lost among the ruins of deceit laid there by the lies of the enemy. We, as God's children of war, must return to the truth by girding our very lives with the belt of conformity. Conforming to God's truth demands a rejection of the lie fed to our souls for too long offering nothing but foul nourishment. It's spiritually necessary that we believe and embrace the power of God's truth. Turn in your Bible to the following passages of scripture regarding truth. Note what you learn about truth from each and how vital it is to our lives. Ask who, what, when, where, why and how to help open up the text of God's Word. Look for the benefits of walking in truth and how it affects one's life with and without it. Note any warnings given concerning God's Truth.

I Kings 2:4

_____

_____

I Kings 3:6

_____

_____

Psalm 15:1-2

_____

_____

Psalm 40:10-11

_____

_____

Proverbs 3:3

_____

Ephesians 4:24-25

_____

_____

Last one, dear student, I Timothy 3:15. Note what the body of Christ is concerning truth.

_____

_____

The church, the body of Christ, is the pillar and support of truth! Do you see the beauty in this truth and how it correlates to the belt of truth and what a belt does? A belt supports and upholds! The belt of truth is agreeing with God by yielding to the responsibility He has given us concerning His truth. This brings us to our Principle for today.

*P*RINCIPLE

GOD'S TRUTH IS THE FOUNDATION AND SUPPORT OF MY LIFE

Truth is that faithful watchdog over our lives. According to Psalm 51:6, what does God desire to see within us?

_____

_____

In John 8:22, Jesus spoke of the power of truth in one's life saying; "You shall know the truth and the truth shall set you free." Truth has the power to deliver and to release us from the grip of darkness and into the Kingdom of Light. Truth is the lifeline of our victory; apart from truth, we are mere captives bound by the shackles of lies. Most of all God desires to find truth in the innermost being of our soul. Truth is safe and planted in the inner recesses of our beings. It is pure and beautiful in the eyes of God. We must never sacrifice truth for honor, for comfort or conformity, and never exchange it for our own version of truth. We live in a time of universal deceit where lies are regarded as justifiable tools to get ahead, for political gain, for forging relationships, for acquiring financial success, and even for revenge and retaliation. Lies are spoken openly and behind closed doors with no shame or reverence of God. Truth is an inconvenience for ungodliness. I want us to read aloud our principle once more and follow it up with our Life Application.

Principle: Because God's truth is the foundation and support of my life then...

Life Application

I Am Unstable Without It

II Timothy 4: 3 & 4 reveals that in later times people will fall away from sound doctrine (truth) and will pay attention to myths because they want to be taught according to their own desires. They will turn their ears away from truth. Without truth, we have no foundation, no support in life. What would a life that lacked a foundation and support be like? What problems do you think they might have?

_____

_____

_____

_____

I want to show you one more very powerful passage of scripture concerning truth and the consequences that come when it is abandoned or rejected. Turn in your Bible to Isaiah 59:12-15 and read through these verses. According to verse 15 of this passage, what happens when one turns from truth?

_____

_____

When truth is missing, our protection is missing as well because we become prey when truth is missing. Truth is everything for the spiritual warrior because it is the support of the other armor pieces and it holds the weapons of the warrior. We must belt ourselves with the very truth of God by building everything in life upon it. We must guard it, search for it, and align our lives with it to ensure stability in all things. Take everything you hear, everything you are taught, all your circumstances, all you encounter, every emotion and relationship, and lay it out beside the truth of God's Word. If it doesn't line up, beloved, then you must not receive it or allow it to remain in your life. What do you use to hold your life together? What are you depending on to steady yourself when faced with difficult circumstances? Are you looking to others for support? Are you relying on your financial soundness, your health or job to secure your future? What happens when and if these things are taken from you?

This is the radiance of God's truth: ***It never changes.*** It will be there when you are old and gray and it will be your securing force in a world so uncertain. God's truth will never fail you nor will it ever forsake you. It will never mislead you and in the darkest of times, it will be a beacon of light illumining the path of hope. Truth is the nourishment of the soul, bringing life where there was only death. Every day we must take up the belt of truth and wrap ourselves about with it. Having declared our need for truth, we then walk every day with God's truth placed before us.

So, as we begin to close our time together today, let me leave you with this question:

What belt are you wearing?

_____

Read through the prayer with me for girding ourselves about with truth.

Father, I confess Your Word is Truth and it is the Light for every path You would have me to take. I declare my commitment unto Your Holy Truth today, inclining my ears to receive it. I will walk in Your Truth today, girding my mind and soul as a protective covering to shield me from the world. I will not build my life upon anything but Your Truth knowing my support is found nowhere else. It is my anchor of soul for every turbulent time.
Amen

Thank you for your diligence to finish our first day of study this week. This is our memory verse for today and we will end by reading through it several times. Much love for you! I'll look for you on Day Two.

MEMORY VERSE
Psalm 25:5

Lead me in Your truth and teach me, For You are the God of my salvation; For You I wait all the day.

Day Two

The most ornate part of a soldier's armor many times was his breastplate. A Roman soldier's breastplate was made of brilliant metals, usually of iron and polished brass. They usually weighed around 40 to 50 lbs. The giant Goliath's breastplate weighed 125 1bs and was no doubt very elaborate. Whenever captured by the sun's rays the breastplate was beautiful. It would reflect the light of the sun with such brilliance and glory that many times the enemy's eyes were blinded by its splendor. When an entire army was arrayed in the sunlight, the display was dazzling and very intimidating to the enemy. Remember Day One of our study; "Dress for success?" Well, the Roman's did just that, the reflection from their armor sent many a foe retreating from the fight. Light is powerful!

This breastplate was attached to the belt by leather thongs passed through rings on the bottom to keep it solidly attached. It was anchored to the belt, and it was above the belt. The belt had to be put on first, then the breastplate. One key area the soldier's breastplate protected was the heart, not to mention other vital organs. It is this vital organ that we want to look at today, dear student. When the enemy wants to deal a fatal blow, it is at the heart he will make his aim to strike. We must understand the necessity of the breastplate in order to protect our heart against spiritual fatality. Pray before you begin and then we'll jump right in today.

Let's begin by reading through Ephesians 6:10-18 as way of review and making it more permanent. Hold up your right hand and proclaim your victory by naming the five pieces of our armor! You can peek back at Day One if you need to! Once you've named these five pieces, write them down in the spaces provided.

1._____

2._____

3._____.

4._____

5._____

I'm so proud of you! On Day One of our study this week, we looked intently at the belt of truth. This belt is what ties everything else in place and holds the weapons securely in the place they need to be. According to this next piece; what kind of breastplate is it? What is it referred to as in Ephesians 6? The breastplate of...?

1. _____

Turn to your Word Windows Section and locate the meaning for the words, *"Breastplate"* and *"Righteousness"*. Record your findings in the space given.

Breastplate

_____

_____

Righteousness

_____

_____

Remember that these pieces, although physically used, are given to us as representation of our spiritual armor. Based on your word studies, what kind of breastplate would this be? How would it assist us in everyday spiritual of life?

_____

_____

What does a breastplate do for the soldier in battle?

_____

_____

If you answered "protect the heart", then you are right, precious student! The breastplate was worn over the shoulders and it covered the front and the backside of the soldier. It attached to the belt which kept the breastplate in place. Without the breastplate, you have no protection over your heart, the most vital organ in the body! Every other organ in the body can be perfect, but without a heart it does them no good. We're given a picture here of righteousness as the protection for the heart of man. The belt of truth declares what's right but it needs the other pieces to put it in to action.

The breastplate of righteousness is the living truth that you have confessed so boldly by wrapping it around your waste. I want us to understand the reality of righteousness in our lives by looking up and reading the following passages of scripture. Note what you learn about righteousness from each. See how righteousness is seen, obtained, and the rewards of it. Interrogate each verse, asking your questions to help open up the fountains of insight.

Psalm 17:15

_____

_____

Psalm 5:8

_____

_____

Psalm 45:7

_____

_____

I Peter 2:24

_____

_____

I John 3:7-10

_____

_____

_____

_____

Revelation 19:11. How does Jesus wage war?

_____

_____

_____

_____

The breastplate of righteousness makes proclamation of lifestyle! There is no excuse for the abandonment of holiness, even when engaging in war with an unholy enemy. Our enemy's character should never dictate ours. When we put on the belt of truth, we are proclaiming what we believe in. When we put on the breastplate of Righteousness, we are living what we believe.

This brings us to our Principle for today.

$\mathcal{P}$RINCIPLE

RIGHTEOUSNESS IS DECLARED THROUGH CHARACTER

Jesus wages war in righteousness and we are to follow suit. This is the difference between warring in the flesh and warring in the spirit. The Righteous One cannot wage war in unrighteousness and be wearing the Belt of Truth! No righteousness means no truth! *If we are not walking in truth by living righteously, then we are not warring for the Kingdom of God.* Hard truth, but true, none the less, beloved. Read the following verse that speaks of God and answer the questions that follow.

Isaiah 59:17

"He put on righteousness like a breastplate, and a helmet of salvation on His head; and He put on garments of vengeance for clothing and wrapped Himself with zeal as a mantle."

What garments did God put on? What does this tell us that God was going to do?

_____

_____

What did God put on before putting on garments of vengeance?

_____

_____

What a powerful reality of God we see here, just as we saw with Jesus. Even in the day that God pours forth His wrath upon sin, He will still put on the breastplate of righteousness before going into battle. God, Who has every right to do as He pleases, still raises up the standard of righteousness and adorns Himself about before stepping out to judge, even when the enemy is undeserving. We, in the Lord's army, must follow the General in charge by warring a good fight, which is done in righteousness! This is why it is vital to place this breastplate over our hearts, so we will fight well and honor God.

I want us to see why it is so important that we protect our heart in righteousness. Look at the following verses and note what you see about the heart of man from each. Take interest in why it is important to protect our heart and the dangers that can come into our lives without it.

Deuteronomy 13:17

_____

_____

Psalm 84:5

_____

_____

Psalm 86:11

_____

_____

Psalm 119:11 & 80

_____

_____

Hebrews 3:12

_____

_____

Hebrews 10:22

_____

_____

How vulnerable the heart is and how prone it is to wander from the truth of God's Word. Knowing this, God forewarned us, calling for us to take up and put on the full armor of His weaponry that we will be able to stand firm against every attack of the enemy. We must barricade our heart behind the holiness of God, aligning our lives with His every word. This is what it means to put on the breastplate of righteousness; lining up our walk with our talk! Walking with that breastplate upon our hearts means living it out in our lives. Let's read aloud the Principle we have learned today and then follow it with our Life Application.

Principle: Righteousness is declared through character then…

LIFE APPLICATION

CHARACTER BECOMES THE VOICE OF OUR FAITH

Turn to Proverbs 4:23 and note what it tells us about the heart.

_____

_____

Jeremiah 17:9 paints a picture for us of the power of the heart to destroy. Listen to his words: ***"The heart is deceitful above all things, and desperately wicked: who can know it?"*** How needy our hearts are for a Breastplate of Righteousness to come and cover us with its saving power. We must never underestimate the power of our heart to destroy us, apart from God's standard. What have you placed before your heart, beloved? How are you guarding your heart? We must put on the righteousness of God, beloved, or our hearts will run wild to the path of destruction.

Read your prayer aloud, beloved, and let your ears hear truth.

My Confession

I confess my heart is desperately wicked and I cannot even know it. It will mislead me and take me captive in the land of sin. I take up the Breastplate of Righteousness and I claim it as my standard. I will not allow anything unholy to carve a path in my life by infiltrating my heart. My heart belongs to You, Lord and I will not give it to another. I cannot leave it to itself or it will self destruct. I proclaim through my life that I will wage war on the righteous path, no matter how unholy my enemy.

Amen

Review your memory verse and we'll call it a day. I appreciate you so very much.

Day Three

My older sister, Susan, was somewhat of an entrepreneur when she was growing up. When she was in junior high, she decided to set up a lemonade and cookie stand right outside of our home at the end of the driveway. It was in the middle of the summer, just right for selling nice cool lemonade to the hot and thirsty kids of the neighborhood. She recruited help from her best friend and they began to advertise the "grand opening" to anyone who would listen. As the big day approached, I became really excited as I saw them baking cookies, mixing the lemonade and drawing the signs. I had saved my allowance to spend at the big day and I thought the big day would never come.

The morning of the grand opening, Susan began to tease me that I had better hurry up and get out there because everything was going to be sold out. My mom had made me take a shower and clean my room, before I was allowed to go out there. I began to feel a big eight year old panic attack coming on, so I rushed around and quickly got dressed, grabbed my piggy bank and darted out the front door. There was a line all the way down the street and Susan was selling lemonade and cookies like crazy. I ran as fast as my legs would take me and took my place out front. All of a sudden, everyone started laughing hysterically and I had not a clue except they were pointing at me. I suddenly understood when I looked down and saw that in my rush out the door, I forgot one very important article of clothing: MY PANTS! Needless to say, I was scared for years!! I decided that day our family really needed to move.

This dress fatality would prove to be the first in a long line of many that would come! I've had many clothing mishaps and, sad to say, there is not time nor enough room to pen them here! I'll save the really embarrassing ones of my adult years for another time. All kidding aside, have you ever dressed for an occasion and forgotten something or dressed inappropriately for an event? What we wear or what we aren't wearing can make a huge difference depending on the circumstances, amen? Our armor for Spiritual Warfare is very specific when it comes to what we are to wear. On Day One and Two of our study this week, we began looking at what we should wear in order to be successful in battle. Today, we'll continue that same route of study. If you haven't already, take time to stop and pray, asking God for His blessing and wisdom to be poured out upon you as you study His Word.

Hold up your right hand and proclaim the armor God gives to His children of war. We know that we begin by putting on the belt of truth, because it's the belt that holds everything up! Second, we learned that we are to put on the breastplate of righteousness, by living out the truth that we have proclaimed we believe in. Let's read through our passage of Ephesians 6:10-18 and find what our next piece of armor is. Write it out in the space provided for you.

_____

The shoes of peace are the next piece of armor that we must put on, beloved. These shoes are no ordinary shoes because God says they are the "Preparation of the gospel of peace". We can't buy these in our local shoe store! So special are these that they prepare the way for the coming of the m: gospel, which brings peace. In your own words, describe what you think the word, *"Gospel"* means.

Gospel

_____

_____

Before we can understand what it means to shod our feet with the preparation of the gospel, we need to first understand what the gospel is. To help us, turn to the following passages of scripture and write down what you learn about the gospel. Note what it is and what it does.

Matthew 4:23

_____

_____

Mark 16:15

_____

_____

Acts 14:14-15

_____

_____

Acts 20:24 (this is my life verse, beloved, and it has a very special meaning in my heart)

_____

_____

Romans 1:16

_____

_____

208

Ephesians 1:13

_____

_____

Colossians 1:5

_____

_____

II Timothy 1:9-10

_____

_____

Word Windows and locate the meaning for the word, *"Gospel"*. Record your findings in the space provided for you.

Gospel

_____

_____

Based on what you've seen thus far, what do you think the gospel entails? What is it, and what are we to do with it? What does it do for the hearer, etc.?

_____

_____

_____

The gospel is God's message of redemption found only in Jesus Christ, His only begotten Son. In the gospel message we are told the story of Jesus and how He came to earth by becoming a man. He lived on the earth for approximately 33 years and He performed many signs and miracles among people, so they would believe in Him as their Savior. He was delivered over to be beaten and flogged, and then crucified upon a cross. While He was on the cross, God took every sin of every soul past, present, and future, and He poured them out on Jesus. There, on that cross, Jesus was judged for the sins of the world, for sins He didn't commit. Because of His sacrifice, we are declared as forgiven, righteous and holy! We can now live with Him in Heaven for all of eternity. This is the good news of the gospel. Anyone can receive this good news and the promise of forgiveness and eternity that it gives. This brings us to our Principle for today.

$\mathcal{P}$RINCIPLE

THE GOSPEL GIVES LIFE BY REMOVING THE STING OF DEATH

Death has lost its power because it can no longer hold captive those who have believed upon Jesus Christ as their Lord and Savior! Them are slapping words!

Read I Corinthians 15:54-55 and note what has happened to death.

_____

_____

To understand what the gospel is, is great but, God calls us to shod our feet with it. Turn to your Word Windows Section and find the meaning for the word, *"Shod"*. Write it in the space given.

Shod

_____

_____

Read the following two verses and note what you see about feet! Yes, that's right; you guessed it, we're studying feet.

Nahum 1:15

_____

_____

Romans 10:14-15

_____

_____

Based on what we've read, how might we shod our feet with the preparation of the gospel?

_____

_____

_____

Because of sin, we lost our peace with God by becoming His enemy. The gospel gives mankind a way to have that peace again with God. How might this be used as armor in warfare, beloved? Give this some thought and see what God impresses upon your heart and mind.

_____

_____

_____

A Roman Solidier had two pair of sandals. One pair was ornate and worn in everyday activities, but the other was thicker and was solely for wearing in battle. The soldier's shoes were a vital part of his armor. His war shoes had jagged edges sticking out from the sides and underneath to help keep him from stumbling in combat. These shoes gave him sure footing to keep him from falling. They were made with the intent of keeping him balanced on his feet when doing hand-to- hand combat. His war shoes literally allowed him to hold his position! This is what we need to take in and understand, beloved. The gospel is our stability!

Let's read aloud our Principle again and then follow it with our Life Application for today.

Principle: Because the Gospel gives life by removing the sting of death ...

LIFE APPLICATION

I HAVE SURE FOOTING IN THE LAND OF THE LIVING

Sure footing is found only in the Gospel of Jesus Christ. We must not settle for unsure footing, going through life stumbling as those who do not know Christ. Our feet must be shod with the saving power of Jesus; they must run swiftly to declare it upon the mountain tops. I want to leave you with one more question.

How might we shod our feet with the preparation of the gospel? What are ways that we do this?

_____

_____

_____

_____

_____

_____

Review your memory verse for this week and we'll call it a day.

Day Four

"Above All, taking up the Shield of Faith that you may be able to extinguish all the fiery darts of the devil".
Ephesians 6:16

Welcome to our last day together this week! You've made it through, mighty warrior, and I am thanking God for my every remembrance of you and the faithfulness you have shown. Take time to bow your knee with me, as I am pausing to do now on your behalf, and seek the Lord God for wisdom, insight, and understanding beyond your years. Beseech Him to change you, grow you, empty you, and fill you with more of Him and more of His power. How vital our time is when we rest before the Lord, seeking Him first. When you have finished your time with God, then we'll begin by reading through Ephesians 6:10-18. Hold up your right hand and declare aloud the five pieces of your armor that we've been learning! Remember, these are our defensive weapons! When you are comfortable reciting these, jump into your study!

The world demands evidence of God, yet marks of existence are clearly substantiated whenever we take the time to take note of creation. The earth pulsates with the life-giving power of Creator God, Himself; the One True Living God! His existence is undeniable.

Robert Jas-trow, one of the world's leading astronomers, founder and director of the Goddard Space Institute, and an agnostic, shocked his colleagues by admitting, at a national conference of the Association for the Advancement of Science, that "contrary to the articles of faith in the scientific profession, evidence seems to demand an intelligent Creator of the universe."
Chuck Missler

God has given us everything we need to build a shield of faith declaring He is real! Whether this astronomer realized it or not, the shield of faith was lifted up to the glory of God by speaking the obvious! I amen Mr. Jas-trow by declaring, YES! There is an intelligent Creator of the universe and His name is Jehovah God, the Almighty, The Ancient of Days, The Eternal One, Holy and Just, Who is Sovereign and forever the Faithful One! Blessed and powerful is the shield of faith to pierce the darkness of unbelief, eradicate the mockery of agnostics and disgrace the atheist. It is, without question, the unexplainable force of power in the lives of God's children when it is raised in the battlefields of the Lord.

We have come to my favorite piece of spiritual armor simply because of its representation and the force it yields in the lives of every follower of Christ. This most priceless piece of armor will be our focus today. I want to give you some details concerning the shield that the Roman soldier carried into battle.

The Shield

The Roman shield was about 4 ft. high and about 2 1/2 feet wide. These military shields were typically made of wood, covered on the outside with thick leather, which not only deadened the shock of the missile, but protected the frame of the shield from the fire-tipped darts used in the artillery of the ancients. The shield was the maneuverable part of the warrior's armor. It was designed to protect him from arrows and javelins, flaming and otherwise. If the shield had any holes or damage, survival would depend upon fixing it before entering the battle, certainly not during! The diligent warrior would direct his energies to its repair as part of his pre-engagement preparations.

Go back through Ephesians 6:10-18 and note everything you see about the shield of faith. What are we told about this piece of armor and what are we to do with it?

_____

_____

Are we told anything special about this armor, what we are to do with it that maybe we are not told to do with the other pieces? Explain.

_____

_____

In addition to all, *"take up the shield of faith"*. This piece of armor is positioned above the other pieces. This should send a red flag up the pole of our "need to know"! This piece of armor is vital to the others being able to do what they should do for the warrior. So we might better understand, turn to your Word Windows Section and locate the definition for the word, ***"Shield"*** and record your findings.

Shield

_____

_____

What kind of shield is this? Fill in the blank, beloved!

Shield of _____

Because this is a shield of faith, we know that is not something we can make or conjure up ourselves. It is found in the spirit realm, from the spirit of the Living God. Why do you think this shield of faith might be something we take up above all the other armor?

_____

_____

We've looked at faith in one of our previous lessons, but it's vital that we understand how faith operates as a shield in our life. To help us with this, take a minute and locate the definition for *"Faith"* in your Word Windows Section and record your findings.

Faith

_____

_____

_____

To help shed more light on this principle, turn to and read three verses that give us marvelous truth regarding the power of faith. Write what you note from each one out beside the verse.

I John 5:4

_____

_____

I Peter 1:3-5

_____

_____

Hebrews 11:6

_____

In the light of the verses we've just looked at, answer the following questions.

Where does our victory come from?

_____

How are we to approach God?

_____

How do we overcome?

_____

_____

In the light of Ephesians 6:10-18, what does the shield of faith protect us from?

_____

The shield of faith is needed to protect us from the "flaming arrows" or as the King James identifies them, the "fiery darts" of the enemy. Often times, we suffer the sting of his arrows, his darts, simply because we did not identify his ammunition! Locate the meaning of the words, *"Flaming"* and *"Arrow"* in your Word Windows Section and record your findings.

Flaming

_____

_____

Arrow

_____

_____

What does this tell us about the attacks of the enemy, knowing he uses no ordinary arrows but fiery ones? Think about what fire does.

_____

Fiery Darts

Fire is consuming and destroys everything in its path. Fire has an insatiable appetite, beloved, and it is never quenched. It is these flaming arrows that we absolutely must learn to identify and place the shield of faith up as a barrier between our life and the attack of the enemy. One way to identify these is to realize that Satan's attacks, his flaming arrows, will always head straight to our emotional corridor. He aims at the emotions in order to gain an open door to the spirit. Satan triumphs in the realm of our imaginations, once he's gained access. Satan is the master of conjuring up imaginary scenes, and replays events like a horror movie; He has the ability to make things so real and vivid as if they were taking place at that moment. He does this through our dreams at night or our daydreams in the light. He lies in wait for an unguarded mind to idle in the stillness of life, and then he makes his move. He comes to us disguised as an angel of light, seemingly beautiful, good and even wise. These *"flaming arrows of the evil one"* may come in the form of depression, feelings of inadequacy, unexpected fears, anxieties, panic attacks, numbness or a dreary feeling, depleting our joy for no reason. Satan will plant the seed of doubt and then feed the voice of rationalization.

We must learn to identify the source himself, the devil, and it is he whispering to us. He can and will communicate destructive thoughts to minds because our thoughts are the train tracks that run straight to one stop; emotion central. He will convince us that these thoughts are our own because they came from our feelings! Have you ever had a thought come out of nowhere like a big ole cannon ball and it just blows you away? Concerning your thoughts, have you asked yourself, "Where did that come from?" How could I think such a thing! It goes against everything we hold to be true. That is when we must recognize that it really is not us, but thoughts planted in our mind by the evil one.

So, what is God's military provision for His beloved troops? It is a mighty shield welded in strength, soldered with faith. This God- given shield is given to protect and sustain us; to hold us steady and keep us on course. In order to take up this shield, we must place our trust in the One Who welded it for us. We cannot position ourselves behind someone if we do not trust in him for protection. God is faithful, He has promised never to leave us nor forsake us. He goes before us in holy fire, burning a path for us to follow. We must place our absolute trust in Him or we will not follow or depend on Him. We will be found without the shield in the day of fire. This brings us to our principle for today.

PRINCIPLE

THE SHIELD OF FAITH IS OUR CONFESSION OF TRUST IN GOD

If you struggle with trust, then you can know that your shield of faith is going to have some holes in it that you are going to have to repair spiritually. Let me share one other powerful thing about a soldier's shield and what they can do with it. When moving forward in battle, the soldiers would form what is called the *"Tortoise Formation"*. Twenty–seven soldiers would combine their shields together having six in front and seven in each of three rows behind forming a solid block. The soldiers on the outside edge would interlock their shield vertically. The ones on the inside would form the roof with their shields. This would form a virtually impenetrable walking tank, thus the name "Tortoise", because of the shell of defense it formed over them. They would even test this in training sessions by driving a chariot over the top of one of their Tortoise formations to make sure it held.

One of the beautiful truths we see emerging from this battle strategy is the need to work together as one body. If one shield is strong, then a group of them is even more powerful! If one shield is missing from the "spiritual tank", then this creates a vulnerable spot that the enemy can penetrate. How many holes exist today in the body of Christ, giving the enemy access into the lives of God's people simply because we are not working together in unity and in the power God has given to us? The most beautiful display of the bride of Christ is unity in motion, shoulder-to-shoulder, advancing across the battlefields, *standing firm in one spirit, with one mind striving together for the faith of the gospel* (Philippians 1:27). Look at the following verses and note what you learn about trusting in God from each. Ask yourself if these verses describe your heart. Meditate upon the character of God.

Psalm 18:30-35

_____

_____

Psalm 28:7

_____

_____

Psalm 76:1-3

_____

_____

Psalm 91:4

_____

The body of Christ must learn to trust in the Lord, their God, and not in programs, finances, talents, a pastor, or any other thing. The shields are put up one at a time, beloved warrior, and I pray it will begin with you and with me. Without trust, there is no shield of faith available to us. This brings us to our Life Application today. As usual, I've listed the principle for you and I encourage you to read it through first and then follow it with the Life Application.

Principle: Because the Shield of Faith is our confession of trust in God then…

LIFE APPLICATION

IF I AM NOT TRUSTING IN GOD, I AM WITHOUT A SHIELD

God is the Shield, beloved! We just saw this magnificent truth in the scriptures we just looked at. We could easily insert the words this way: Take up the God of your faith and be absolutely sound in our doctrine. God is the Shield, beloved, but He cannot be our faith! You and I have a choice to make;place our trust in Him as when we first came to salvation or we can continue to walk according to the flesh, in our strength and without hope. Let me ask you a heartfelt question.

Do you trust in the shield of your faith? Explain how and why or why not.

_____

_____

_____

_____

_____

We are making our way through the armor and there is so much more to come! Let's look back over all that the Lord has shown us this week by filling in our Week in Review Chart. Write in the Principle and Life Application to the corresponding day and allow these truths to wave over your soul like fresh waters.

OUR WEEK IN REVIEW

Day One

Principle:
Life Application:

Day Two

Principle:
Life Application:

Day Three

Principle:
Life Application:

Day Four

Principle:
Life Application:

Write out your memory verse for this week to make sure you have it sealed in your heart. Include the scripture reference as well.

MEMORY VERSE

_____

_____

_____

_____

Let's read our confession of truth aloud, declaring our acceptance of the word God has given to us this week.

MY CONFESSION OF TRUTH

I confess, O Lord, that I am a soldier in the army of the Living God. I am strong in You and You make me to stand strong upon the front lines of the spiritual battle field. I confess that Your Word is truth. I take up your truth and wrap it round about my waist, believing it to be my holding power. I proclaim my righteousness is in the breastplate of Jesus, Whom I have given over my heart and hide it there behind His holiness. I step into the shoes of peace; the peace I have with God and in God through the blood of Jesus Christ. I take up the blessed shield of faith and lift it up as a covering of protection for me and my fellow comrades. Shoulder to shoulder I will war next to my sisters in Christ and there take my stand with them until the trumpet of victory is heard.

We will close our week together with our Personal Evaluation questions. Take your time with these and pour out your honesty before the Lord, knowing He will bless You for it.

Personal Evaluation

Are you standing for truth even when it's uncomfortable? Are there any areas that you sacrifice truth by turning away or ignoring error?

_____

_____

_____

Are you living what you believe or are you hiding behind the breastplate of the world? What does your breastplate declare?

_____

_____

_____

Have you shod your feet with the gospel, bringing peace to the lost?

_____

_____

_____

Do you trust God?

_____

_____

_____

Are you striving together with your brothers and sisters in Christ or are you striving against them?

_____

_____

_____

How have you been defending yourself against the enemy?

_____

_____

_____

With this I'll say goodbye for now. The armor for the child of God is necessary for victorious living. I'll see you in our lesson time together.
Much love for you, Pam

Session Notes

LESSON SEVEN

Fully Armed and Loaded

Fully Armed and Loaded!

Day One

The soldier's duty is one of valor and a stance imbedded in the belief that the fight for freedom is worthy of death. With great resolve of heart and burdened soul, they march on into the belly of the beast, into the shadow of the valley of war knowing for this they were born. It is from this heart resolution that tenacity is ignited and a warrior is born. To understand war, we must see the heart of the soldier who engages the battlefields of life and death. I want to share with you the combat soldier's prayer written by Gary Jacobson in 1999. It moves my heart deeply. I believe we can see the heart of the warrior in the words he penned.

> *This combat soldier's prayer,*
> *Who has served his time in Hell,*
> *Is may we learn the lessons of war well,*
> *That we not doom future generations,*
> *The same old tales of horror to tell,*
> *To endure what in youth they see mistakenly as glory.*
> *Oh God, do not let our children*
> *Repeat the same old story.*
>
> *Make it so that America's babies live to grow old*
> *In this land of the free and the bold.*
> *Help us throw off the shackles of hate that bind*
> *And grow old in a life of a peaceful kind.*
>
> *Teach us that there is no glory in war,*
> *Nor honor there that brave men should not abhor.*
> *Teach us instead, one for another our brothers to love.*
> *Shower us with thine Celestial message from above,*
> *That we plant seeds of peace evermore*
> *And make war-no-more!*
>
> *But if I should die on some far, far away battlefield*
> *Know I answered the call*
> *For a grand principle of freedom to yield.*
> *My fervent prayer is that death*
> *May not have been in vain*
> *Fighting for peace and right for the world to attain.*

My brothers, American roses standing by my side
On alien soil dying
In the summer of my youthful pride
All the leaves around me falling,

Now I'm lying here still, in sunshine and in shadow,
Longing to hear, "brother next door, I love you so."
For moldering in the soft ground below,
I feel you living and loving in the world above me
standing tall because I fought that you might be...
Oh look ye down now,
And tell me you still think of me
Honor my red blood, spilt that others might stand free.

Tell me that I did not give my all for you in vain
That brothers and sisters do not look upon my sacrifice
With hateful,
Or even worse,
Uncaring disdain.

Do not forget me when my valley's hushed
And white with snow,
Grass growing green in the summer of my meadow
Help me see the peace I lived and died for grow.

Make my lonely grave richer,
Sweeter be...
Make this truly,
"The land of the free
and the home of the brave,"
I gave my life to save
That I might too, lie eternally,
Forever free...

A soldier never knows where his battle shoes will take him or the visitation day of death, but ready he must be to spill his blood upon the soil of peace so the oppressed may go free. It is for freedom they labor and surrender their lives, not counting the cost. Freedom is the difference that separates us from life and death, peace and turmoil, strength and weakness, and honor and disgrace. The battlefields, though stained with the blood of God's saints of old, lie desolate, ravaged by the enemy; the warrior is missing. The trumpet has sounded and the call has gone forth to rally the troops, to take up the armor and with sword in hand, rush the enemy line. With that said, take time to pray, seeking God's wisdom and blessings upon your study time and then let's jump right in!

Let's hold up our left hand and name out loud our five unseen resistances! Once you've finished, record these five in the space provided for you! We must never forget these, beloved. These five are our identification of our very present, unseen enemy, the tactics and forces he uses against us.

1._____

2._____

3._____

4._____

5. _____

God has given us these five specific, unseen resistances so we will not be deceived, having the ability to label our attacks for what they are. Knowing these gives us the power and ability to stand firm against each and every attack because we are calling them what they are. But God expects more from us, and wants more from us than just awareness. He charges us to battle and entrusts us with His armor; we are His armor bearers and with that comes the responsibility to train with, and become proficient in the use of His weaponry. In the light of this, we began learning our five defensive weapons. We learned four of these in our study last week. Today, we'll continue to the last one. For the sake of review, read through Ephesians 6:10-18, which is located in the back of your study book. Write out the first four pieces of armor that we have studied thus far.

1._____

2._____

3._____

4._____

God never, absolutely never, leaves His child defenseless in His battlefield. As you read through our passage of scripture in Ephesians 6, what piece of armor did you see next that we found in our defensive armor? Record it in the space provided. This will be our fifth piece of defensive armor.

5. _____

The helmet of salvation! What purpose do you think a helmet might serve in battle? What does it do for a soldier?

_____

_____

The importance of the head does not need much convincing. A soldier can survive broken bones, but a broken head is many times a signed death certificate. In the Garden of Eden, (Genesis 3) God addresses the serpent (Satan) regarding his enticing Eve to eat from the forbidden tree. When sentencing him to death, God spoke these words regarding the deathblow Jesus would inflict upon Satan at the cross; *"He shall bruise you on the head!"* The head is the place of life and death, beloved! We must protect our heads in battle because one fatal blow could bring death in our life. The helmet worn by Roman soldiers was made of metal and designed to protect the head, face, and neck without blocking vision. Centurions and other officers wore crests on their helmets, so that their men could see them and follow them into battle. How many soldiers today in the Lord's battlefields are being separated from their unit because the helmet of salvation is no longer visible upon the lands of war? If the helmet is lacking from the soldiers head, it not only exposes the soldier to possible fatality, but it puts his comrades at risk as well.

The apostle Paul, the writer of Ephesians, sheds more light on the helmet of salvation for us in I Thessalonians 5:8, a passage we have looked at previously. Locate this verse in your Bible and see it with fresh eyes. Write it out, word for word. This is also our memory verse for this week! So, you are already getting a head start on memorizing it!

MEMORY VERSE

I Thessalonians 5:8

_____

_____

_____

How does Paul describe the soldier's helmet in this passage of scripture?

_____

_____

God unveils the life- protecting power of the believers' helmet with one word: ***"HOPE"***. He tells us that the helmet is the *"hope of salvation"*. This is no ordinary word for hope that is used here. Turn to your Word Windows Section and retrieve the meaning for this powerful word!

Hope

_____

_____

You can take many things from a person's life, no matter how painful, no matter how costly, and there remains the opportunity to recover and continue living. But take away a person's hope, life will not remain long. Hope is the heartbeat of the soul. Strip the heart of hope and the beat will fade slowly until it is no longer heard. The hope of salvation is for the head. It covers our minds, intellect, and reasoning. Hope, as we have seen, has a very different meaning from what we use the word for in the normal sense of the word. When we say, "I hope I get the promotion", the phrase itself implies doubt and an expectation that we have absolutely no control over. Hope from God's perspective is much more powerful. Hope is one of the three essentials. Read aloud the following scripture and listen to what it reveals about this powerhouse called HOPE.

"And now these three remain: faith, hope and love. But the greatest of these is love. "

1 Corinthians 13:13

Faith, hope and love are all indispensable and crucial for every believer because they remain, beloved; they are steadfast and eternal. Faith is an attribute of the heart. Because of the marvel of this gift treasured in the heart of God's children, we can still put our faith in Him even though we may not understand all that He is doing. Hope is different from faith; it is not of the heart, it is of the mind. Hope covers the head of God's children. Hope is our helmet, our protective covering in battle. I want us to see the power of this hope that is unveiled for us in the Word of God. Turn to the following passages of scripture and glean truth from God's definition of hope. Note the source of hope and its importance.

Titus 1:2-3

_____

_____

Colossians 1:22-23

_____

_____

Our hope is based on the eternal life of God; it is extended to us in the gospel. The gospel is the giver of this hope, precious one, and we are the blessed recipients! Continue looking at the blessings we receive from hope as revealed in the following verses. These are some slapping verses so get your hands ready for action! I want you to see what a powerhouse hope is to us who have put our faith in Jesus Christ.

THE POWERHOUSE OF HOPE

Psalm 25:3-5

_____

_____

Psalm 33:20-22

_____

_____

Psalm 119:81

_____

_____

Isaiah 40:31

_____

_____

Hebrews 6:17-19

_____

_____

Hope provides us with an anchor, something we can cling unto with our very soul (faith, intellect and emotions.) Faith needs hope to sustain it. The helmet of salvation gives God's children utmost hope as we do battle with the enemy. Remember, the word, "hope", infers a certain expectation of a future blessing. This thought given is that there are aspects of our salvation that are yet future. We have a future home in heaven, a future glorification, a new body, every tear wiped away, unspeakable joy, the presence of God, seeing the face of Jesus, rewards, mansions, golden streets to trod upon, and more and more importantly with complete assurance. Hope allows no shred of doubt or uncertainty. This brings us to our Principle for today

*P*RINCIPLE

HOPE ANCHORS OUR SOUL IN THE FUTURE WE HAVE WITH GOD

The scheme of the devil is to rob every child of God of their future. We saw this in the Garden of Eden when Eve and Adam lost the right to eat of the tree of life and live forever because of Satan's enticement to sin. The helmet of salvation, this headdress of hope, allows us to view warfare through the eyes of eternity. If we do not have it on, Satan can cause us to give up, quit, despair, and become discouraged by whispering words to us like; "You're having to wait too long! This fight is lasting too long! This isn't working, you may as well quit, etc."

The helmet of salvation enables us to maintain total confidence in victory, no matter how long the battle may seem to last here on earth. We have a salvation that is certain and eternal! We cannot be ultimately defeated! There is absolutely no room for discouragement in light of the helmet of salvation! What does hope in the Lord mean to your life, beloved? Write out a brief testimony of the hope you have that anoints your head!

My Hope

_____

_____

_____

_____

_____

It is one thing to know about our helmet, but it's another to know how to lay hold of that hope in order to put it on! Hope is enlarged the same way faith is; it grows stronger with use. An amazing thing happens when we study God's Word; with study comes understanding, and with understanding faith, and with faith, comes a greater hope in God's ability to fulfill His promises. When the helmet of salvation becomes very strong, we can anchor our very soul to it. The hope of eternal life protects our mind from the relentless assault inflicted by the enemy. A child of God, who has this anchoring hope, will be sustained in peace during times of confusion. There will be strength to overcome temptations of the fleeting pleasures of sin. Choosing eternity over the temporary things of the world will not be a challenge. It's this hope of soul that casts out every anxious thought and washes away all fear. When the enemy shoots the fiery arrows of despair, doubt or temptation at our minds, we will not yield, because hope will have secured our defenses.

Look up these two scriptures and write down what you see concerning the stability of God's child. Note where it comes from.

Isaiah 33:6

_____

_____

Colossians 2:5

_____

_____

What an anchor! So, what does hope that anchors our future in God mean for us, beloved one?

LIFE APPLICATION

STABILITY OF TIMES

Ephesians 4:13 tells us that we are no longer to be tossed to and fro in regards to our faith no matter how turbulent the times are. We have an anchor, precious warrior, an anchor sure and able to stand against every torrent of evil. Our anchor will never fail us because hope never disappoints. Let me share a scripture bountiful with God's promise of security for the heart anchored in hope, for the mind dressed with the helmet of salvation. Read it aloud. There are two verses that I want us to see before we finish our time together today. Look at these and write down what you are told about the one who hopes in the Lord! What are the benefits of having hope based upon these verses?

Psalm 31:24

_____

_____

Psalm 130:7

_____

_____

Without salvation, we have no hope, precious one, but because we do, we are never hopeless. God gave us the helmet of salvation to protect our minds from doubt, confusion, and every lofty thing that would raise itself up against the knowledge of Who He is. With our mind braced for war, we must cover our thoughts with this blessed hope knowing that we have a future with God; therefore, we have no need to fear the present. I pray you will stand in the truths we have been shown this week knowing that the helmet of your salvation, your helmet of hope, is the stability of your times because it is your anchor of soul. Take courage, daughter, because our hope is in Him and He will never disappoint us. I pray, O how I pray for you right now as I type these words, asking God to make you a woman of divine hope! Settle for nothing less, dear one. It is the soul of hope that dawns, gracing the victor's crown upon their brow.

You have completed your right hand of defensive weaponry, beloved, and I'm so proud of you. See if you can recite all five! Take a few minutes as we close our time together and say these five aloud.

Rest now and I'll see you on Day Two of our study.

Day Two

The Word of God is timeless, inerrant, infallible, living, active, refining, holy and sharper than any sword, even having two edges! An all- powerful and all- knowing God, harnessed Who He is and His heart toward us and penned it upon pages deemed as holy, pure, and redemptive. His word sustains the weary soul, endowing it with hope for every situation. It is a fountain of living waters quenching every thirst of life. Hidden within its parchments are the ancient paths that lead to the hill of the Almighty. Inside every page is the very breath of God extending grace to all who will receive Him into their heart. It is the beacon of safety lighting the way to glory for the dying saint. It crosses every racial boundary, defies all other religions, is not restrained by social status, and the pit of failure is never so deep that it cannot pull the longing soul out of its depths. By it, we live and we die, we march on to victory no matter the foe. The Word of God is the only force that can shut the mouth of the roaring lion and send the demons of hell running!

Your opinion and your value of God's Word will determine the outcome of your battles. You cannot go to war defenseless and unarmed. There is no need to clothe ourselves with safety if we have no weapon to advance us across the battlefield. This is why God gave us His word, precious one! The word of God is more powerful and sustaining than we could ever know. It is our lifeline in this world and our crowning glory in the next. We have much to see today, so with all of that said, take time to pray seeking the favor of the Word Himself and then we'll begin.

Write out in your own words what the Word of God means to you. Describe how it affects your life and how much time you devote to it. Explain why you feel the way you do?

_____

_____

_____

Lift up your right hand of power and authority and speak out loud your five defensive weapons. Once you have said these, write them out in the order they were given to us in the spaces provided for you.

1._____

2._____

3._____

4._____

5. _____

What do these five defensive pieces of armor mean to the Christian?

_____

_____

How many of these are you clothed with right now as you are doing your study? Explain your answer.

_____

_____

Read through Ephesians 6:10-18 as a refresher and write down what follows the helmet of salvation.

_____

What are we told the sword of the spirit is?

_____

_____

What would a soldier use a sword for? Why would they need one? What is the sword used for in battle?

_____

_____

_____

What kind of sword are we told this one is? In other words, what is it made of? The sword of what?

_____

The sword of the spirit! This obviously is not an ordinary sword. Can you hold a spirit in your hand? Do you think this is a literal sword? Explain your answer.

_____

_____

What makes this sword unique is what it is made of. It is not forged from the blacksmith's fire, nor is it made of any earthen metal. It is a sword of the spirit. It is the Holy Spirit, Himself that bears the arm of offense for you and me. Turn to your Word Windows Section and locate the definition for the word, *"Sword"* and record your findings in the space provided for you.

Sword

_____

_____

According to Matthew 10:34, what did Jesus bring to earth?

_____

_____

We're never told that Jesus drew or even carried a sword. In fact, when Peter wanted to charge the whole Roman coalition, Jesus restrained him from doing so, but not before Peter could get one good blow in taking off the ear of a slave. Jesus was against violence while He lived upon the earth, but yet, He said He came to bring a sword. If Jesus carried no sword yet He tells us he came to earth to bring a sword, He must be speaking of something other than a sword that we can physically pick up. Many have said He was speaking of future time when He will return to this earth to wage war against the wicked. That may be so, but it is clear that Jesus was speaking of why He came the first time. He was not using future tense. So, what kind of sword could He be speaking of? Look up the following verses and note what you learn about Jesus and who He spoke of.

Matthew 1:20

_____

_____

Mark 1:8

_____

_____

John 20:22

_____

_____

Acts 1:8

_____

_____

John 14:18-27

_____

_____

In Ephesians 6, what are we told to do with the sword of the spirit?

_____

_____

God instructs us to take the helmet of salvation and the sword of the spirit. I purposely saved this word study until today because I want us to see it in the light of the sword of the spirit! Turn to your Word Windows Section and locate the meaning for the word, *"Take"* and write it out.

Take

_____

_____

_____

Based on this word study, what does it mean to take the helmet of salvation and the sword of the spirit?

_____

_____

The sword of the spirit is the Word of God, beloved, but this sword we are told belongs to the hand of the Spirit, Himself! He will not use a weapon crafted by human hands lest the sword boasts against the very one that brought it from the fire. There is but one sword worthy to find its place in the hand of the Holy One; His Word. Every word, every line and page bears His imprint: a blade wielded with a Heavenly parchment. This holy weaponry, the flesh can never take up on its own terms. Proclamations for it are a Holy Sword fit for the divine purpose of the One Who breathed it into existence. The Sword and its Maker are One; they are inseparable just as God intended them to be. This brings us to our Principle for today.

*P*RINCIPLE

THE WORD OF GOD IS THE SWORD OF THE HOLY SPIRIT!

While it's true, the Holy Spirit is compassionate bringing comfort to God's children, He's the faithful guide and patient teacher. Though He is as quiet and gentle as the breeze rustling through the trees and peaceful as a dove descending upon our Savior, He brands a very fatal weapon of power. This powerful weapon of God's Word merits further study, beloved. Read the following passages of scripture and note what you see about the Word of God! Note its power, its use and ministry. Ask your interrogating questions; ***who, what, when, where, why and how***

Acts 19:20

_____

–_____

I Thessalonians 1:8

_____

_____

I Timothy 4:2

_____

Titus 1:9

_____

_____

Read the following passage from Hebrews that is typed out for you. Make a list of all that the Word of God is and what it does. Take your time with this! The text is typed out for you.

Hebrews 4:12

For the word of God is living and active and sharper than any two-edged sword,

and piercing as far as the division of soul and spirit, of both joints and marrow,

and able to judge the thoughts and intentions of the heart.

The Sword of The Word of God

_____

_____

_____

_____

_____

_____

_____

How many sides can cut from this divine sword of God's Word? Describe the blade, beloved, as given to us in Hebrews?

_____

_____

Now, beloved of God, let's hold up our right hand and declare with each raised finger the five offensive weapons of armorGod has given to us. Once you have said these five offensive armor pieces, clasp your hand to make a fist as if you have taken hold of a sword and add this to your memorization! This will be our taking up the sword of the Spirit! Amen!

The sword of the Spirit is two-edged; it is all edge, beloved, and no matter which direction it strikes, it can wound and destroy. There is no flat part of the sword of the Spirit; therefore, the one who takes it in hand must be careful how it is used. We cannot use the Word of God to cut others without the cut of the blade facing us! This sword was not wielded for the hand of the hypocrite. This sword we can use against every carnal desire; pride, deceit, jealousy, bitterness, unforgiveness, dishonesty, thievery, unbelieving heart and every fear. Make no bones about it; the sharpness of this sword can penetrate to the marrow of the bone for both the enemy and the handler. What a humbling truth for us, precious warrior. The same blade that will slay the enemy upon the battlefield bringing swift death is the same holy blade that will bring us down as well. Though the Word of God is the Sword of the Holy Spirit…

PRINCIPLE: BECAUSE THE WORD OF GOD IS THE SWORD OF THE HOLY SPIRIT!

LIFE APPLICATION

IT STRIKES AT MY HEART JUST AS IT DOES MY ENEMY

When we draw the sword of the Word from the sheaf of the Holy Spirit, we are ever reminded that though one blade is aimed at the enemy the other is aimed at me. Holiness will not tolerate hypocrisy. The warrior that takes the sword of the Spirit in hand, the living Word of God must do so with fear and trembling. God gave us a double blade to keep us pure and submissive to the One to Whom the sword belongs. It is not for the coward or the calloused, but for the pure in heart; taking every word into their own lives before they ever dare to take it up in war. I want us to close out our time together today by sharing with you a mighty charge given to the warrior of God, as seen in Ephesians 6:17; written by Charles Spurgeon.

> *"No man was ever holy by a happy chance. Infinite damage may be done by carelessness; but no man ever won life's battle by it. To let things go on as they please is to let them bear us down to hell. We have no orders to be quiet, and take matters easily. The one note that rings out from the text is this:—TAKE THE SWORD! TAKE THE SWORD! No longer is it, talk and debate! No longer is it, parley and compromise! The word of thunder is— Take the sword. The Captain's voice is clear as a trumpet—Take the sword! No Christian man here will have been obedient to our text unless with clear, sharp, and decisive firmness, courage, and resolve, he takes the sword. We must go to heaven sword in hand, all the way. "TAKE THE SWORD." On this command I would enlarge. May the Holy Spirit help me?"*

And so I would bestow unto you, faithful one of God, TAKE UP THE SWORD! God bless your efforts of study. Press on; we are almost there to the end! See you on Day Three.

Day Three

One of the greatest men of prayer was George Mueller of Bristol, England, who in the **last sixty years** of his life had received from God's hand over seven million dollars through prayer alone. George Mueller never prayed for anything out of his own desires, or even because he felt it was needed for the work of the Lord. He prayed only as it was laid upon his heart to pray, and only then when a promise from God's Word was found to support it. It's been said that he would search the Word of God for days before he presented his petition to God. He would pray with his Bible open to the promise God had given him, and there, lay open before him, with his finger upon that promise, he would plead that promise. George Mueller understood and believed in prevailing prayer! He knew that God was bound to His child and to His promises, for God cannot lie. He never prayed without an open Bible before him.

Prayer pulls the rope down below and the great bell rings above in the ears of God. Some scarcely stir the bell, for they pray so languidly; others give only an occasional jerk at the rope. But he who communicates with heaven is the man who grasps the rope boldly and pulls continuously with all his might."

Charles Spurgeon

We have covered all of the pieces of armor, but there's one act, one responsibility, one privilege, given to the warrior of God that is as vital as any and all the pieces of armor put together: Prayer. Many are lacking victory in their public life because they lack prayer in their private life. This will be our convicting topic of study today, beloved. I warn you ahead of time, when God gives us truth, we are then held accountable to activate that truth in our life, making it a reality. God supports living truth because His Word is living! So, hang in there with me today and faint not…amen? Before you begin, make sure you have prayed first. Let me give you a wonderful prayer that Charles Spurgeon always used when he opened his Bible to study God's Word; May it become your prayer today as well. *"Lord God, let the words leap off the page into my soul; make them vivid, powerful, and fresh to my heart."*

Let's put everything together that we have learned thus far. Hold out your left hand and recite aloud your five unseen resistances! Yes, I know you've done this numerous times but repetition means permanence! I don't want these to fade from your memory when we are finished with this study. Say these over and over again, several times aloud. When you are finished, take the right hand of your authority in Christ Jesus and speak aloud each defensive weapon raising one finger at a time. Once you have your right hand open having recited each defensive weapon, reach out in front of you and close your hand as if you were grabbing a sword and confess the sword of the

Spirit! To make sure we have sealed in our five defensive weapons, write these five out in the space provided for you.

1._____

2._____

3._____

4._____

5. _____

And for good measure, what is your one Offensive Weapon?
_____

You'll thank me for this one day!! LOL. I do so appreciate you and most of all, for putting up with me. You are my happy thought as I write this course! Let's read through our Warfare passage in Ephesians 6:10-18. As you read through these verses, ask the Lord to sear them into your heart and mind, retaining them as a life-saving device. When you have finished your review, write down what we are told to do once we have armed ourselves and taken up the sword of the Spirit?

_____

_____

I want us to see the difference between prayer and petition. To help us accomplish this, turn to your Word Windows Section located in the back of your book and find the meaning for the words, *"Prayer"* and *"Petition"* that is used in Ephesians 6:18. Record your findings next to the corresponding word.

Prayer

_____

_____

_____

Petition

_____

_____

Praying can be an act of worship and an expression of our heart as we cry out to God the needs and desires of our life. But petitions are needs, the desperations of our heart and mind. Both are necessary to warfare in the spirit realm.

According to this passage, how often are we to pray?

_____

We are to pray at all times, beloved. This little word, "all" is loaded with meaning and I want us to see it. Locate the word meaning for *"All"* and write it out in the space provided for you.

All

_____

_____

_____

Who are we to pray for?

_____

_____

How are we to pray? In the what?

_____

Praying in the Spirit is what is needed in Spiritual Warfare. The flesh will never set its affections to the things of God. The Spirit holds the sword, and He is the One Who is needed to pray through us; so we won't pray fleshly prayers that will avail no power to the believer, no matter how long or often they pray. God is not interested in meaningless repetitions, but words spoken from the mouth of the Spirit through your prayers. This is what God's ears are attentive to. Look up the following passages of scripture and note what you learn from each, regarding praying. Look for how often we are to pray, the affects of prayer, the power of prayer and the responsibility, if any to pray.

Nehemiah 4:9

_____

_____

James 5:16

_____

_____

What kind of prayer accomplishes much according to James 5:16?

_____

What kind of person is needed in fervent prayer in order to accomplish much?

_____

Based on this passage of scripture, can you have one without the other to avail in prayer?

_____

_____

Turn to your Word Windows Section and locate the meaning for this word, *"Fervent"* and record your answer in the space given to you.

Fervent

_____

_____

Let's do the same with *"Accomplishes"*. These two words are the secret to a powerful prayer life. This is a secret that Satan will never want God's children to learn. You become a threat to the kingdom of darkness when these two things are present in our praying.

Accomplishes

_____

_____

Let's look inside our prayer closets for a minute; take note of the shape it is in. If I were to open up your prayer closet, beloved, the place where you have set as your prayer place, would I find it worn, stained with tears or filled with cobwebs? Are your knees calloused from kneeling in prayer or is your heart calloused from a lack of prayer? Do you have a designated prayer place at all? Truth is hard, but in order to grow we must first face the truth about ourselves and our lives. Write out a description of your prayer life in the chart provided for you. What is it like, how often do you pray? How long do you pray? For what do you pray, etc..? Answer the questions out to the side of your Prayer Life chart.

MY PRAYER LIFE

What kind of prayer life do you think God desires for you to have?

_____

_____

_____

_____

_____

Do you believe you have that now? If not, explain why and what has kept you from praying or increasing your prayer life?

_____

_____

_____

_____

Turn to Ezekiel 22:28-30 and read this passage noting what is told about the praying soul.

_____

_____

_____

What could God not find?

_____

_____

What are we told that God needed a person to do for the people of the land?

_____

_____

_____

What was coming upon the land and the people if this person was not found?

_____

_____

What does this reveal about the power of prayer?

_____

_____

I want you to see the power of a prayer as shown to us in God's Word. Look up the following passages of scripture and as you read through each one, note the power of prayer and anything else God reveals to you about prayer and what we are to pray for, etc?

I Kings 8:22-54 (this is a lengthy portion but the prayer of Solomon is absolutely beautiful and powerful) Note his position when praying.

_____

_____

_____

I Kings 17:20-24

_____

_____

II Kings 6:15-17

_____

_____

Hebrews 13:8

_____

_____

Ephesians 1:7-8

_____

_____

Philippians 4:6-7

_____

_____

We absolutely cannot make it without prayer, beloved? Without prayer, we are signing our own death warrant to our spiritual life. This brings us to our principle today.

$\mathcal{P}$RINCIPLE

PRAYER IS THE LIFELINE OF EVERY WARRIOR OF GOD

Prayer is the wall God has erected as an altar for His warrior. The wall elevates the altar above the war zone giving God's child a view from above. It is the place dedicated by God as the place of ascension for the saints' petitions; it is the gateway unto His holy hill that opens for the cry of his children. Turn to the following passages of scripture and note what you learn from each about this wall of prayer. Note the heart of God for this wall.

Ezekiel 22:30

_____

_____

Isaiah 49:16

_____

_____

Isaiah 62:6-7

_____

_____

The watchman is the prayer warrior who has taken his place upon the walls above the cities of God crying out night and day, morning and evening, until the petitions have been given. But one thing that must not escape our notice, precious student; this valiant prayer warrior does not take his stand upon the wall without his armor or sword in hand. Remember that the armor is put on first, then the sword clasped tightly in the right hand; only then can the warrior climb the wall of prayer. Read through the principle again and then follow it with the benefit.

Principle: Because Prayer is the lifeline of every warrior then…

LIFE APPLICATION

THE WARRIOR MUST DECIDE IF HE WANTS TO LIVE OR DIE

God has put within our reach the power of life and death in the spiritual realm of warfare. But you and I have to make the choice, beloved. No one can fill your place on the wall of prayer. God tells us that "your walls are continually before me." Why would we not want to occupy the place that is before His eyes? Jesus ask His disciples the night of His arrest; "Could you not keep watch with me for one hour?" Is He speaking this to your heart today? Would He find you praying? How do you think God would want you to respond to your lesson time today? Write out a confession of truth and how you will respond. This will close out our time together today.

My Response

What a great student you are! See you on Day Four.

Day Four

We are constantly bombarded with new diets, new treatments and programs designed to give us a whole new body, a whole new YOU! We can turn to Jenny Craig with no charge for losing the first twenty pounds (what a deal that is, huh?) There's Doctor Oz, The Biggest Loser, Weight Watchers, Nutra System, and if that's not enough there's always Botox! We can grow our eyelashes fuller and longer than when we were, well, too young to remember. We can poof our lips up, permanently remove that unwanted facial hair, have a tan without ever stepping outside, whiten our teeth and vista la resistance, we can even grow our hair through magical extensions. We can have a fake everything and be voted one of America's most beautiful people! What a world we live in! The irony is that we look for real change through temporary fixes. We know we have to change, but we don't know why or how!

When God brought us into the world, He left room for improvement in our inner being; improvement that can only come from and through Him. If we want strength, we will never have it apart from Him; if we fall down we need Him to get back up. When we sin, forgiveness is only found in Him, and our need to be loved is fulfilled in His arms. This is God's design, beloved, to need Him more than life itself. A soldier is confident upon the battlefield only when they know who they are, when they are trained and when they trust in the heart of their general. We can only march one step at a time and each step takes trust. It's this dependency that we will look at today in the Word of God. Take time to pray and then, we will begin today's journey through the pages of God's Word.

Read through Ephesians 6:10-18 as way of review and look with new eyes at all the armor and weaponry God has given to us for battle. See the command to stand firm and be strong, allowing the provision of His weaponry to lift us up above all self-doubt, fear and failure. As we survey the goodness of our God in protecting His children and His call to bear arms, taking our stand upon the walls of His altar, we can know that God has seen to it that we have all that we need to succeed in battle. As is our practice, beloved warrior, let's hold up our left hand and identify our five unseen resistances! If we never identify the attacker, we will be overcome! Second, once we have identified our attacker, we must take our stand fully armed with sword in hand. Hold up your right hand of power and authority and declare yourself armed, as you call out with confidence your five defensive weapons ending with the sword! Once you have declared these five pieces of armor (defensive ones), fill them in on the hand chart given to you, writing your pieces of armor upon each finger beginning with the thumb. We must, at any cost, learn to identify our protective armor and above all, learn to take up the sword of the Spirit, which is the Word of God.

Think with me for a moment about the sword. Eph 6:17 tells us to take the helmet of salvation with the sword of the Spirit. We know what this word "take" means so where does that put our sword? Check which one you think applies.

- ❑ In The Sheath (the soldiers' holder)
- ❑ In the Hand of the warrior

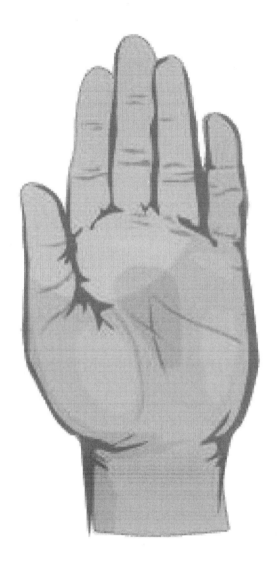

I believe the picture we are given is one of the sword being in the drawn position! This follows suit with the soldier who is on the alert knowing that his adversary, the devil, is roaming around like a roaring lion, seeking to devour him. So many soldiers are being fatally wounded spiritually and emotionally because they have never drawn the sword of the Spirit out of the sheath! A drawn sword means a soldier is armed and ready to defend and offend, if necessary. Our Bibles lay dusty in the covers (sheaths) or in the back seat of our car during the week, left there from the previous Sunday service without a thought until the next week rolls around. No soldier goes about in battle without his sword! How smart would that be? Let me share some verses with you today that reveal the cutting power of the sword of God's Word. To aid us in this process, I want us to do something so simple, but very practical and powerful. This spiritual exercise will yield great rewards in the battlefield if you make this a habit in warfare. It's Spiritual Warfare training day! We want to learn to first draw our sword and then secondly, learn how to use it for the cutting weapon that it is. Read these aloud and see first the drawing with the sword and then the cutting with the sword. Simple exercise but oh, the power!

Drawing The Sword

Philippians 4:13 - "I can do all things through Christ Who strengthens me"

Cutting With The Sword

CONFESSION: I AM STRONG IN THE STRENGTH OF THE LORD!

Drawing The Sword

Isaiah 54:17 – "No weapon that is formed against you will prosper"

Cutting With The Sword

CONFESSION: SATAN, EVERY SCHEME OF YOURS WILL FAIL!

Drawing The Sword

Psalm 27:3 – "Though a host encamp against me, My heart will not fear; Though war arise against me, In spite of this I shall be confident."

Cutting With The Sword

CONFESSION: SATAN, I AM NOT AFRAID OF YOU, I AM CONFIDENT BECAUSE JESUS HAS ALREADY DECLARED VICTORY OVER YOU!

Drawing The Sword

John 10:29 – ""My Father, who has given them to Me, is greater than all; and no one is able to **snatch** them out of the Father's hand."

Cutting With The Sword

CONFESSION: I BELONG TO JESUS, SATAN, AND HE WILL NEVER LET YOU HAVE ME!

Drawing The Sword

John 15:13 – "Greater love has no one than this, that one lay down his life for his friends."

Cutting With The Sword

CONFESSION: JESUS DOES LOVE ME, SATAN BECAUSE HE LAID DOWN HIS LIFE FOR ME.

Drawing The Sword

I John 4:4 – You are from God, little children, and have overcome them; because **greater** is He who is in you than he who is in the world.

Cutting With The Sword

CONFESSION: SATAN, HEAR ME; THE OVERCOMER RESIDES IN ME AND HE HAS DEFEATED YOU BECAUSE HE IS GREATER!

Can you begin to see how the Word of God is Your Sword, beloved? It cuts the enemy down while also cutting right to the heart of your being, opening up the storehouse of life pouring in the faith and power that comes from hearing God's Word! Now, I want to give you an assignment to do on your own. Find three Scriptures and do the same thing I have done. When you find a scripture you want to use, write it in the space under "drawing the sword". Then, write out, in our own words, a statement of truth under "cutting with the sword." You can use verses from this week's study or any of the previous weeks or you can search out new ones on your own! You may have a life verse you want to do this with. Whichever ones you choose will be a benefit.

Drawing The Sword

_____

_____

Cutting With The Sword
CONFESSION: _____

_____

Drawing The Sword

_____

_____

Cutting With The Sword
CONFESSION: _____

_____

Drawing The Sword

_____

_____

Cutting With The Sword
CONFESSION: _____

_____

How does this make you feel in your spirit to do this exercise?

_____

_____

_____

I want us to see how Jesus did this in His own life against the devil. Read the following passage of scripture that is typed out for you and underline every response that the Lord gives to Satan, using a red colored pencil! Note how He drew the sword and how He cut with the sword. Once you are finished, write out how Satan responded and how this attack ended.

Luke 4:1-14

1. Jesus, full of the Holy Spirit, returned from the Jordan and was led around by the Spirit in the wilderness

2. for forty days, being tempted by the devil. And He ate nothing during those days, and when they had ended, He became hungry.

3. And the devil said to Him, "If You are the Son of God, tell this stone to become bread."

4. And Jesus answered him, "It is written, 'MAN SHALL NOT LIVE ON BREAD ALONE.'"

5. And he led Him up and showed Him all the kingdoms of the world in a moment of time.

6. And the devil said to Him, "I will give You all this domain and its glory; for it has been handed over to me, and I give it to whomever I wish.

7. "Therefore if You worship before me, it shall all be Yours."

8. Jesus answered him, "It is written, 'YOU SHALL WORSHIP THE LORD YOUR GOD AND SERVE HIM ONLY.'"

9. And he led Him to Jerusalem and had Him stand on the pinnacle of the temple, and said to Him, "If You are the Son of God, throw Yourself down from here;

10. for it is written, 'HE WILL COMMAND HIS ANGELS CONCERNING YOU TO GUARD YOU,'

11. and, 'ON their HANDS THEY WILL BEAR YOU UP, SO THAT YOU WILL NOT STRIKE YOUR FOOT AGAINST A STONE.'"

12. And Jesus answered and said to him, "It is said, 'YOU SHALL NOT PUT THE LORD YOUR GOD TO THE TEST.'"

13. When the devil had finished every temptation, he left Him until an opportune time.

14. And Jesus returned to Galilee in the power of the Spirit, and news about Him spread through all the surrounding district.

How did it end for Satan?

_____

_____

How did it end for Jesus?

_____

_____

What sword did Jesus use to fight the attack of Satan?

_____

_____

How did it wound Satan?

_____

_____

The Holy Spirit's sword in battle is the Word of God. It is two- edged and able to pierce to the marrow. Why would we draw anything else to try and fight the adversary with! The overcomer has shown us the way, given us the training manual and the weapon to be victorious against every kind of attack, even when we are weak and vulnerable just as Jesus was at the time of His attack. This brings us to our Principle for today, precious student.

*P*RINCIPLE

THE WORD OF GOD ARMS ME AND DISARMS SATAN

The Word of God is your power to bear arms against your enemy. We cannot arm ourselves with the Word of God if we do not draw it from its cover and open it up daily. This is why Bible study is so vital to our walk and growth in the Lord. Look at the following verses and note what you learn from each.

I Corinthians 1:18

_____

_____

II Corinthians 6:4-7 (this one should be familiar, note what it says about the Word of Truth)

_____

_____

Titus 1:8-9 (note how the Word was used)

_____

_____

 I John 2:14

_____

_____

How we must have the Word of God richly dwelling within us so we may combat every attack. Apart from God's Word, we have no defense and we have no offense. Where is your heart for God's word in your life right now? Is it a priority? Is it a necessity of life for you? How I pray that it is. Without it you are unarmed, vulnerable and without help. How often we ask God to deliver us from Satan's attack when He has given us the weapon to use against him? If the Word of God arms me, then it disarms Satan.

LIFE APPLICATION

THE WORD IS MY SOURCE OF LIFE IN THE BATTLEFIELD

What is your source for living? What is your source for victory? How do you stand against the enemy's attacks? What do you do when you are afraid, lonely, anxious, depressed? How can you overcome temptation and the lusts of the flesh? Let me start your heart by meditating on the things we've learned.

With all God has taught us, we must look back and reflect on the Principles and Life Applications. Go back and survey all that He has shown us and fill them in on the corresponding week.

OUR WEEK IN REVIEW

Day One

Principle:

Life Application:

Day Two

Principle:

Life Application:

Day Three

Principle
:
Life Application:

Day Four

Principle:

Life Application:

One more thing, beloved! I want to give you a warfare prayer, claiming all that God has given us. You can have it before you always. I pray you will read it daily!

A Prayer for the Woman of War

Father God, exalted in the throne room of Heaven, You are mighty to save, protect and advance me in the day of battle. You are a warrior, O God, and I, Your armor bearer. I follow You into battle clothed with the bravery You have woven for me. I take up the belt of Your truth and gird myself about the waist. I hold to Your truth and walk accordingly. Your truth is life unto my bones.

I put on the breastplate of the righteousness I have in Jesus Christ. I confess my need for forgiveness and apart from Jesus; I am ever sinful in Thy sight. I am righteous in Him and in Him alone. I will live according to His righteousness and not my own works.

I am in agreement with You, Father, so I take up my shield of faith hiding myself behind in the trust I have placed in You and the truth of Your word. Without faith, I cannot please You. Enlarge my shield today and keep me following behind You in the greatness of the faith You give me. Reflect the radiance of Your glory upon my shield in the battlefield, letting the enemy know I march behind the Living God, the God of Abraham, Jacob and Isaac. Make my shield fireproof and extinguish every scheme and plot sent to rob me of life.

I shod my feet of clay with the peace of the Gospel that saved my soul. I will walk in the security of my salvation in You because Jesus has made me to be at peace with You. Order every step I take and make my feet of clay beautiful for every life I walk into today. Let me trod upon the pathway of the dying soul that I may bring them the good news of Jesus Christ before it's too late. Give my steps an urgency to pursue the lost souls.

I take the helmet of my Salvation and cover my mind with its saving power. Protect me from every destructive thought sent from the enemy and let it not penetrate my helmet. I am saved, sealed and will, someday, be delivered into your eternal presence. Make my helmet a holy sifter, straining out every thought that is not of you. I give you the keys to my mind O God, stand watch at its doors today.

I reach into the holy sheath that is girded about my God and there, I draw forth the Sword of Your Word. It is sharper than any two-edged sword. I raise it unto the face of my enemy and I renounce his power and authority in my life and the life of my family. I will not turn to the right nor the left of the Living Word of my God. Satan, the Lord rebukes you this day! You have no authority over me, in me or through me. I will not run from the battle but stand today, fully armed with God's armor with sword in hand, drawn ready for action.

And to every evil spirit, every world force of darkness, every spirit of wickedness in the heavenly places within the sound of my voice, hear me now: I am the armor bearer of the Almighty God, The God of all Gods, the God of you and me. I stand behind Him and the shield and power of His hand. You are under His feet, your days are numbered, and the eternal lake of fire is waiting for you. I am victorious in Jesus. You have no influence on me today and you have no power over me. In the name of Jesus I cancel every appointment you and your leader, Lucifer, will try to make with me or my family today.

I am a mighty warrior, a woman of war, fully clothed with the militant armor of Jehovah. I am armed and ready for battle. I walk on holy ground that has been seared with the fire of the Holy One, Himself. Nothing and no one shall come nigh my tent today! Because my God is with me, I will fear no evil! In the name of the Mighty One Himself, Jesus Christ, I pray,

Amen

Personal Evaluation

What are you shielding your mind with?

_____

_____

_____

_____

_____

How are you fighting your battles?

_____

_____

_____

_____

_____

How does God want you to change your prayer life? Why should you?

_____

_____

_____

_____

_____

How important is the Word of God in our lives?

_____

_____

_____

_____

_____

What should you do with what God has taught you this week?

_____

_____

_____

_____

_____

Thank you for hanging in there this week and staying the course. We have one more week to finish our journey. How I pray that you will be steadfast to the end. God is training up warriors of valor and mighty in battle. Let's take our stand upon the wall, fully armed with sword in hand.

Love to you precious one,
Pam

Session Notes

LESSON EIGHT

The Authority of the Believer

The Authority of the Believer

"Behold, I have given you authority to tread on serpents and scorpions, and over all the power of the enemy, and nothing will injure you."
Luke 10:19

Day One

For the rest of your life, one of the most important Scriptural truths you'll ever consider will be what you study this week in God's Word. Before we can be of use upon the earth, we must have the mind of heaven. What the mind embraces, the will obeys. When we learn to set our mind at the right hand of God, the Father accepting who we are, we will walk in accordance with His Word clothed in the power and might of His armor. We must choose, as an act of sheer faith to declare; ***"Lord, I accept my position!"*** This is more than a mere mental assent; it births action. It is this living confession that inscribes the battle line upon the warfront proclaiming victory before the march ever begins. The world lies in the desperation of darkness in need of women and men who fear no one but God; people who will not vacillate in their belief, even when the cost is great, refusing to sacrifice truth for pleasure or acceptance.

We've been journeying through the pages of God's eternal, inerrant Word feasting upon the life changing principles of Spiritual Warfare. The foundation of Spiritual Warfare has been laid and week-by-week, God has built upon that foundation through the truths He has shown us. It comes down to this empowered warrior of God; what do we do with all we have learned? How do we live according to His word? We know the armor He has provided for each of us to use in spiritual battle but what authority do we have over the enemy, if any? Do we have the power to cast out demons, dispel the darkness, conquer territories, or even rebuke the devil? What rights has God given to His children? We must know the answers if we are ever going to trod the path of victory! It is these truths that we want to glean from God's Word this week as we close out our Woman of War study! Let's begin with our prayer time, seeking God's blessing upon our study time.

Read through Ephesians 6:10-18 as way of marvelous review! I want us to hold up our left hand and declare aloud our five unseen resistances! Once you are finished, write these out in the order that they are given to us!

1._____

2._____

3._____

4._____

5._____

Wonderful job! Now, let's hold up the right hand of authority, the right hand that symbolizes our power and recite our five defensive weapons! Once you declared these aloud, take time to write them out just as you did your unseen resistances. List them in the order we learned them from God's Word.

1._____

2._____

3._____

4._____

5._____

Now close your right hand like you are grasping the weapon of truth! Shout out your offensive weapon, beloved, and then write it out in the space provided for you!

_____

What is your sword of the Spirit?

_____

With our armor in place and sword in hand recognizing the enemy, what does God also tell us to do once the sword is taken up?

_____

_____

With all of this weaponry, this armor and prayer, what do you think God expects of us in battle? What are our responsibilities?

_____

_____

_____

When someone enlists in a branch of the armed forces, they are sent to a training center where they will undergo six weeks of vigorous, gut-wrenching training lovingly referred to as, "boot camp." After graduating from boot camp, they anxiously await their assignment; their orders. Once these orders are given, they hasten to go and occupy the area of the earth inscribed upon their assignment papers. Just as a soldier receives his or her orders, so we as God's children receive ours from Him. We can go through all the training, get all the equipment, weapons, ammunition, etc., but until we embark to carry out our marching orders, our training and weaponry are meaningless. Marching orders let the soldier know what they need to do; it's what a soldier anxiously waits for. They understand they were trained and equipped for one purpose and one purpose only; to fulfill the order given to them by the commander.

Well, beloved, the Lord gave each of us marching orders! This will be our focus of study today that will launch us into the rest of our study days as well. Turn to your Text Section in the back of your book and there locate the passage of scripture for Luke 19:1-27. Read through these verses one time to gain an understanding of the events that are taking place. Once you've finished our reading assignment, go back through this passage of scripture, only this time, mark every reference to the nobleman by drawing a purple crown over each one. Remember to mark every pronoun that refers to him as well. When you have finished your markings, go back and revisit each purple crown and note what you learned about this nobleman. I encourage you to ask your interrogating questions such as; who, what, when, where, why and how to open up truth. Compile a list of truths concerning the nobleman in the chart provided for you.

THE NOBLEMAN

_____

_____

_____

_____

_____

Where was the nobleman going and why was he going there?

_____

_____

What did he give to his servants before he left?

_____

What orders/instructions did the nobleman give to his servants?

_____

Write out the specific orders the nobleman gave to his servants before he left as we are told in Luke 19:13.

Orders Given in Luke 19:13

_____

The nobleman told his servants to *"occupy until I come"*. Turn to your Word Windows Section and locate the meaning for the word, **"Occupy",** and record your findings in the appropriate space.

Occupy

_____

_____

_____

In light of your word study, what do you think the nobleman was telling his servants when he entrusted them with his money and told them to "occupy until I come?"

_____

_____

_____

We're going to come back to this term "occupy" in just a minute, so hang on! I want us to stop and take in what Jesus speaks about in this passage. In verse 11, we are told why Jesus shared the parable He did. What subject was Jesus speaking about when He began to tell this parable? What did the people believe about the kingdom of God?

_____

_____

The nation of Israel believed that the kingdom of God was coming immediately. To help them understand that the kingdom of God was not coming in an instant, but only when the King had finished securing for Himself a kingdom, He shared this parable. A parable is a story with hidden meaning for the listener. It always has a target audience in mind! Jesus was speaking in reference

268

to the kingdom of Heaven; His kingdom. If you'll remember, he was visiting a man's home. What was this man's name?

_____

Go back through our study passage of Luke and mark every reference to Zacchaeus by drawing a stick figure over each using the color of your choosing. Make sure you don't skip the pronouns that refer to him. When you are finished, record everything you saw about Zacchaeus from marking the text and record it on your Zacchaeus chart.

Zacchaeus Chart
_____
_____
_____
_____
_____
_____
_____
_____
_____
_____
_____
_____

What did you see about the heart of Zacchaeus?

_____

_____

How did he respond to Jesus when He told him He was coming to his house?

_____

_____

What was his attitude about his sin?

_____

_____

What was the desire of Zacchaeus' heart?

_____

_____

Zacchaeus was a very rich and powerful man, yet his heart is what struck at the heart of Jesus. I want you to see this for yourself. To help you, look up the meaning for *"Zacchaeus"* in your Word Windows Section and note the meaning in the space given.

Zacchaeus

_____

_____

From what you've seen about Zacchaeus, do you think he lived up to his name? Explain your answer.

_____

_____

_____

I believe Jesus was drawn to the purity of Zacchaeus' heart! He wanted to know Jesus and he wanted to be a part of His kingdom. Because of this heart, Jesus came into his home bringing salvation! It is this heart that the king will entrust His treasure to, and assign the duty, "occupy till I come." As we have seen through our word study, occupy is a military term. We are to take what He has entrusted to us and occupy… without wavering. The King establishes and builds His kingdom and while He is away, we are to simply occupy His territory of rulership until He returns. He is the Conqueror; we are the occupiers. This brings us to our principle, today precious student.

*P*RINCIPLE

WE ARE AN OCCUPATIONAL FORCE

How beautifully this lines up with Ephesians chapter 6 when God instructs us to "stand!" We are told to hold our position, standing firm and resisting the devil. Again, the Lord is giving us the same marching orders to "occupy" what belongs to Him, which He has given to us. It is this occupational force that we are commanded to exercise upon the conquered lands of God. Listen carefully, beloved, an occupational force is sent in only when the war is won. The force then simply occupies by stopping any pockets of resistance that may still be lurking in the region. There is a story told of the Right Honorable W.E. Gladstone, when he served as Prime Minister of Great Britain. On one occasion, he brought in to Queen Victoria an important measure for her signature. The queen objected to it, and after some heated discussion, still refused to sign. The Minister of the Crown was unusually urgent and persistent in the cause; *"Your Majesty,"* he said, respectfully but firmly, "you must sign this bill." She turned on him haughtily saying, *"Sir, I am the Queen of England."* Unmoved and without hesitation the statesman answered quietly, *"Your Majesty, I am the people of England."* After some thought, she accepted the situation and affixed her signature to the document.

John MacMillan
Understanding the Authority of the Believer

This story illustrates quite powerfully the question of authority when two opposing powers are in conflict. The believer must be fully aware of the power behind them in order to occupy the territory of the king. The occupational force must acknowledge with full understanding the occupational authority that has been given to them by the King. Jesus would not command us to occupy His territory without giving us the authority to do so. The command to occupy from the king extends the scepter of authority. Authority is delegated power. Its value depends upon the force behind it! To help solidify this understanding, let's go back through our passage of scripture in Luke 19 and circle every reference to the servants of the nobleman, using the color of your choice. Circle also every reference to the "citizens" by drawing a circle but using a different color than you used for the word "servant". Make a list of what you saw as a result of your markings and record your insights in the space given.

Servants of the Nobleman

_____

_____

_____

_____

Citizens of the Nobleman

_____

_____

_____

Which one of the servants would you compare Zacchaeus to in likeness? Explain why.

_____

_____

_____

Look up the word meaning for these two words, **"Servant"** and **"Citizen"** to make sure we fully understand the difference between these two types of people. Record your findings in the designated space.

Servant

_____

_____

_____

Citizens

_____

_____

_____

From what we've seen in this parable that Jesus told, how will the servant and the citizen be judged? What will the difference be, if any?

_____

_____

_____

What should this motivate us to do as His servants?

_____

_____

_____

What is the primary difference between the servant and the citizen?

_____

_____

_____

_____

The servants will give an accountability of what?

_____

_____

Listen, precious warrior, listen with the intent to hear what God's Word is telling us today: we, as His servants will give an account of what He has given to us! What has He given to us for Spiritual Warfare? Think back to all that you have learned and list these out so you can have them before you.

I HAVE BEEN GIVEN FOR SPIRITUAL WARFARE THE FOLLOWING

_____

_____

_____

_____

_____

_____

When your King returns, what will you have to give Him? Will you have added to His kingdom? We are the occupational force, beloved, but with this comes His provision and with His provision comes future accountability. Because we are the occupational force…

*L*IFE *A*PPLICATION

WE ARE NOT RESPONSIBLE FOR SECURING VICTORY ONLY FOR DEFENDING THE CROWN

How many of us continue to lose the battle that has already been won! The Lord never instructed His servants to secure His reign only to defend the right to rule that He gained through His own victory over the enemy of the land. Jesus fought the devil and he lost. Victory is not something we must secure, because our King has already done that. Praise God! Look up Psalm 71:3 and write it out in the space given to you. This will be our memory verse for this week as well so begin to learn it!

Psalm 71:3

_____

_____

_____

As we close our time together today write out a praise unto your King for what He has shown you today!

PRAISE UNTO MY KING

_____

_____

_____

_____

_____

_____

You have worked faithfully today and I thank you for it! I'll see you on Day Two!

Day Two

When Jesus walked the face of the earth, He performed mighty deeds in the lives of people; deeds as the likes which no man had ever seen before. He healed the sick, raised the dead, and even commanded the demons of hell! He triumphed over death, hell, and the grave and no man could contend with His wisdom. So magnificent and awesome was the ministry of Jesus, that the apostle John told his readers in John chapter 21:25 that if they were written down in detail, even the world itself could not contain the books, which were written of them. What does this show us? That the power of Jesus is not bound by, nor can it be contained by space or time, for they are innumerable and indescribable. Because it is boundless and immeasurable, it will never, and can never be, held in the grasp of one person or overtaken by any existing powers, fleshly or spiritual. It is absolutely vital in sustaining your spiritual life, that you know and embrace the truth regarding the matchless power of Jesus Christ!

You will never understand the power you have been given, if you do not know the power of the One, from Whom you received it. We have no authority, no power apart from the source we receive it from. Seeing this from God's Word in its fullness is our goal of study today. I have asked the Lord to allow us to tap the source of truth concerning Jesus' power! Pray before you begin your study, asking God to reveal truth to your soul and a willing spirit to live accordingly. When you have finished praying, we will begin.

Let's begin by reading through Ephesians 6:10-18 as is our norm, engraving its truth a little deeper into the chambers of our heart and mind. Hold up your left hand and declare your five unseen resistances, then follow it with your right hand of defensive weaponry. Grasp the sword and name it aloud, declaring its cutting power so the enemy can hear it. Our enemy needs to be reminded of his position of defeat and we need to declare to our faith our position of victory! This is a fabulously empowering way to start your day, every day! We will look at the power and authority that Jesus gave to His followers. Look at each of the following verses in your Bible and take note of what you learned about the power and authority of Jesus from each, if any, He gives to His followers. Answer any questions that may follow.

Luke 10:17-19

_____

_____

Some believe that Jesus gave authority and power over demons and the devil to the twelve apostles only. Based on this passage from Luke 10, is this true or false? Explain your answer.

_____

_____

John 14:12

_____

_____

_____

What kind of works will the one who has believed in Jesus do?

_____

_____

I John 4:3-4

_____

_____

\Who is the greater One? Where is the greater One?

_____

_____

Mark 9:38-40

_____

_____

Were others, besides the apostles, able to cast out demons? Explain your answer.

_____

_____

Mark 16:14-20

_____

_____

_____

What signs would accompany those who had believed in Jesus? List these signs out in the order they are given. There are five of them! That number five just keeps surfacing in Spiritual Warfare doesn't it?

1._____

2._____

3._____

4._____

5. _____

What was Jesus able to do through them in the world because of their belief?

_____

_____

Where did Jesus go? What did He do when He got there?

_____

_____

How does this compare with the parable we studied in Luke 19 on Day One? Do you see any similarities? Explain your answer, your reasoning.

_____

_____

_____

Jesus defines the authority of His believers, just like the nobleman, by what He gives them. We are given authority over our enemies. We can cast out demons! Let's see what He means when He says "cast". Look up the word meaning for *"Cast"* in your Word Windows Section and record its meaning in the space provided.

Cast

_____

_____

The disciples witnessed Jesus' ascent into heaven. What an experience! But what I want you to see is, that as wonderful and powerful as His ascension must have been, there was something even greater that was witnessed before this event. Turn to Acts 1:3 in your Bible. How many days did Jesus appear to His disciples after His resurrection? What did He do during this time? What do you think His purpose was?

_____

_____

_____

When Jesus rose from the dead, He appeared to His disciples over a period of 40 days. During these forty days, Jesus exposed them to His resurrection power! This is the hidden jewel of spiritual victory over the enemy, over every scheme, every power, every ruler, every spiritual force of wickedness, and world forces of darkness that come against our lives and the lives of our family; understanding and living in the resurrection power of Jesus. This is why Jesus spent forty days with His beloved followers after He rose from the dead! Why not go straight to heaven? Jesus knew that His followers must know, believe, and experience His resurrection power before they could ever fulfill the life He had chosen for them to live. The resurrection power of Jesus is imparted to us at the time we put our faith in Him as Lord and Savior. We've seen clear evidence of this in the verses we've just read. There is a power and an authority that comes at salvation, because Jesus went to the Father in Heaven and released the Holy Spirit to come and indwell every heart of faith. Faith opens the door for Him to come in and set up eternal residency within us.

This brings us to our principle for today.

*P*RINCIPLE

RESURRECTION POWER IS HOUSED WITHIN EVERY BELIEVER

Jesus wanted His followers to know that the greatest knowledge they could possess would be understanding His resurrection power. He took forty days to impart this knowledge to them before He sent them the Holy Spirit. It does no good to have the Holy Spirit of this power, if you do not know the power He has and instills in each of us. Look up the following verse regarding the Holy Spirit and note what power He brings with Him when He indwells the heart of the believer.

Acts 1:8

_____

_____

Acts 4:31

_____

_____

Acts 7:54-55

_____

_____

Acts 10:44

_____

_____

Acts 13:2

_____

_____

Romans 5:5

_____

_____

Romans 15:13

_____

_____

Titus 3:5

_____

_____

Do you see how amazing the Holy Spirit is? He is the resident resurrection power indwelling our lives. With Him comes the power, the miracles, the unexplainable, the healing, the restoration, the endurance, the strength, salvation and every other good gift of God! Housed in us is the same power, the same person that embodied Jesus! We have seen that resurrection power is housed within us, so because this is true then…

LIFE APPLICATION

THE HOUSE IS STRONGER THAN EVERY ENEMY

God tells us in His infallible Word that He built a temple to house His presence and that temple is the heart of the believer. Turn to I Corinthians 6:19-20 in your Bible and write out a description of what it tells you about the Holy Spirit.

_____

_____

This temple is not one built by human hands that no man should gain the glory for it. God's temple is being built, fashioned one stone of truth upon the other supernaturally by the master carpenter ,Himself. Only God can build a temple for Himself to dwell in. This is the gift of every believer, beloved, and with this gift, comes the resurrection power which enables us to do the greater works! Let's close our time together by answering one question. What does God want you to do with the truth He has shown you today? Make this a journal of your convictions that have been drawn from the well of truth. Be honest, open and vulnerable before the Lord.

_____

_____

_____

Review our memory verse for this week and we'll call it a day! Much love to you, beloved student.

Day Three

Do you recognize the power housed within you? How often do you recognize, acknowledge and depend upon the powerhouse God has built in you? Gone are the days of defeat, discouragement, excuse and weakness; they all moved out the day the Holy Spirit moved in. It doesn't matter what battle you are losing, beloved, be it fear, anxiety, anger, malice, jealousy, bitterness, unforgiveness, unfaithfulness, rebellion, lust, etc., losing is nothing more than you and I refusing to "occupy" the land of victory. Remember the weight of the battle is not ours, only the armor. Too often we surrender conquered territory, because we walk off the battlefield of victory in defeat deeming the enemy as an unstoppable force. The authority given to us by the Victor also imparts the power needed to defend the fort, erected above the enemy. It is time to take our stand in the armor given to us and hold the Kings land until He returns. We must before night falls and the battlefields are shadowed in darkness and fear.

What truths we will search out today, beloved, and so I ask you to diligently seek God's blessing and wisdom in prayer before you jump into your study. I am expecting great things from God in our study time today. Let's turn in our Bibles to Genesis 1 and 2 and read through the account of creation. When you have finished, write out what position God put man and woman in regarding His creation. What responsibilities, if any, did He give them?

Adam and Eve

_____

_____

_____

_____

Who did God put in the place of rulership over His creation?

_____

_____

We were designed to rule over God's earth, not to be ruled over by those of the earth. We were placed in the seat of God's authority, given divine instruction to subdue, not to be subdued. God did not create us for bondage, but rather, He created us for rulership! We were given His scepter of authority and His word for obedience; two simple, but life giving truths for mankind. When one of these is out of alignment, the world will take over. Following is a passage of scripture that we will be diving into today. Read through it and once you've finished, write out your thoughts concerning the truths found therein.

Ephesians 1:19-23

"And what is the surpassing greatness of His power toward us who believe. These are in accordance with the working of the strength of His might which He brought about in Christ, when He raised Him from the dead, and seated Him at His right hand in the heavenly places, far above all rule and authority and power and dominion, and every name that is named, not only in this age, but also in the one to come. And He put all things in subjection under His feet, and gave Him as head over all things to the church, which is His body, the fullness of Him who fills all in all"

My Thoughts

Take a colored pencil and going back through these verses, mark every reference to Jesus by drawing a red cross around each, including every pronoun. When you have finished marking the text go back and note everything you learned about Jesus.

JESUS

What did God do through and in Jesus?

_____

_____

_____

Where is Jesus now?

_____

_____

_____

What did God give to Jesus?

_____

_____

_____

What authority did God give to Jesus?

_____

_____

What does this mean to the believer? How does this affect our life?

_____

_____

_____

Where is Jesus' seat?

_____

Following is the tower of authority. Based upon our passage of scripture, fill in the tower of authority as it is described to us. I've started it for you!

Tower of Authority

JESUS

_____

_____

_____

_____

_____

Who does Jesus have authority over in your life?

_____

_____

_____

What is under Jesus' feet?

_____

_____

According to Hebrews 2:6-8, what has He put under your feet as well?

_____

_____

Look up the word meaning in your Word Windows for *"Under"* as used in Ephesians 1 and here. Record you findings.

Under

_____

_____

How does this truth affect your attitude in battle? What response should you have to warfare?

_____

_____

Go back through this passage of scripture and draw a purple triangle around every reference to God. Based upon your markings, what truths did you see about God!

_____

_____

Because of the resurrection power of Jesus, God, the Father seated Him in the seat of authority found only at His right hand. This is the highest seat of power and supreme authority because it has been established as such, by God, Himself. It is this seat that we want to fix our gaze upon today and for life. Typed out for you is a portion of scripture found in the following chapter of Ephesians. Read through this passage and then, write down your first impressions. Focus on the seat you have been placed in!

Ephesians 2:1-8

1. And you were dead in your trespasses and sins,

2. in which you formerly walked according to the course of this world, according to the prince of the power of the air, of the spirit that is now working in the sons of disobedience.

3. Among them we too all formerly lived in the lusts of our flesh, indulging the desires of the flesh and of the mind, and were by nature children of wrath, even as the rest.

4. But God, being rich in mercy, because of His great love with which He loved us,

5. even when we were dead in our transgressions, made us alive together with Christ (by grace you have been saved),

6. and raised us up with Him, and seated us with Him in the heavenly places, in Christ Jesus,

7. so that in the ages to come He might show the surpassing riches of His grace in kindness toward us in Christ Jesus.

8. For by grace you have been saved through faith; and that not of yourselves, it is the gift of God;

My First Impression

_____

_____

_____

_____

Go back through this same passage of scripture, but this time underline every reference to the recipient of this writing, the one who was dead in their trespasses, the one seated with Jesus! Use the color of your choice. When you are finished, write out the truth you see about the one seated with Jesus! Compare it in the light of what we learned about Jesus' seat in the previous chapter. We've looked at these verses before, beloved, but I want us to see them in greater depth today!

Me

_____

_____

_____

_____

Do you know your position in Christ? Based on what we've read in Ephesians, what is your position regarding the enemy, regarding Satan himself?

_____

_____

What does this mean to you in occupying? How does this enable or encourage you to carry out your marching orders?

_____

_____

We have been seated with Jesus! This in itself is powerful enough but then, to know where Jesus is seated is absolutely mind baffling to me. Our finite minds will not be able to lay hold of this fully until we enter the realm of Glory because the power and might of Jesus is something we cannot begin to understand. We can know this though; there is no power greater, higher, or mightier than Him. There is no authority above Him, He answers to no other! He reigns completely, utterly and eternally all because the Father desired it to be so. This brings us to our principle of life today.

*P*RINCIPLE

SPIRITUAL BOLDNESS COMES FROM REALIZING YOUR POSITION IN JESUS CHRIST

What does this mean to your spiritual journey with God? To know that you can be bold for the Lord, that you have been given the seat of boldness? I believe one of the most beneficial spiritual exercises we can do for our faith is to write out a confession of truth when God gives it to us, acknowledging how it applies to our lives. Let's do that now with our Principle of truth concerning our seat of authority. Let's draw forth our Sword of Truth from the sheath and cut truth before our eyes.

My Confession of Truth

Truth dispels the darkness, beloved warrior, and truth puts the enemy to flight. What seat are you occupying? What areas of victory have you abandoned your post in, allowing the enemy to trample upon in flaunting disgrace, before your King? Write out your areas of failure, your areas where you are continuing to lose over and over again? Name them for what they are, precious student? You shall know the truth, and the truth shall set you free. We're going to call these areas of surrender, because these areas have already been won by the King, Himself! We don't lose battles, we only surrender conquered ground. Say this to your heart over and over again, until it settles in over your soul like a cloud of fresh living water. Write out what the Lord reveals to you about your surrendered areas.

My Areas of Surrender

_____

_____

_____

_____

_____

_____

We have been seated in the place of supreme authority with the Supreme One, Himself. We are to hold the scepter of power over every foe! We surrender because we fail to acknowledge and even believe in the rights we receive from the seat, the position we have been given. Read aloud our Principle for today and then follow it with our Life Application.

PRINCIPLE: Spiritual boldness comes from realizing your position in Jesus Christ

LIFE APPLICATION

OCCUPYING THE PLACE OF VICTORY IS GIVEN THROUGH OUR THRONE RIGHTS

We must practice our throne rights daily in order to "occupy until He comes" or we will be found in dishonor upon His arrival. Do you feel you recognize and utilize your throne rights as God's child? Why or why not?

_____

_____

_____

What do you need to change in order to make this a reality in your life on a daily basis?

_____

_____

_____

These are difficult questions, beloved, but we must take a hard look in the mirror until everything that is not of truth is removed through the washing of the water of the Word. Let's close out our day of study together by writing out our memory verse for this week in the space given to you.

MEMORY VERSE

_____

_____

_____

_____

Day Four

Well, we have come to our final day of study together, beloved, warrior of God. Any soldier will tell you that when they are faced with war, they rely heavily on the training they have received. Preparation for them is vital to their making it out alive and for the ability to help save and protect the lives of their comrades. Romans 8:37 tells us that we are "more than conquerors." It wasn't enough for God, that you and I, be conquerors, He desired for us to be MORE than conquerors! We can compare this truth to a soldier who went out to war to fight the greatest battle ever waged. He put his life on the line because of what was at stake; freedom from oppression and bondage. The war was fierce and the soldier was fighting upon the front line of the battle. There upon the soil of war- ravaged land, his blood was spilled out; fighting for the deliverance of all those who could not deliver themselves. His body was war torn, bruised and broken, but he died doing what he was sent to do. But, the war was not in vain, for as He was going down, He struck the enemy with the fierce blow of death. What sacrifice, what honor and deliverance!

As the gun fire ceased to be heard, the sound of victory erupted from the darkness as the sun began to rise. There is no sweeter sound than the cry of the captive who has been set free. The cheer of freedom swells from the blood- stained fields of war, enveloping death with life once again. But there is more. The fields are unveiled beneath the canopy of light that has risen upon the horizon. The spoils of the enemy are laid bare before the victors and it is more than we could ever have imagined. Their commander sounds the trumpet declaring the victory secure, and the charge is given to rush the land, to lay hold of the fruits given from the battle. It has all been worth it, even the life of their fallen comrade who secured their victory.

In Psalms 23:5, the psalmist declares to each of us that God sets a table before us in the presence of our enemies. Jesus rushed the front line for us and defeated the devil, but it cost Him His life. From the grave came the mighty warrior's declaration to us, His comrades; *"Enjoy the spoils of war, take the inheritance I have left for you at my passing."* We enjoy the inheritance that came out of the war that Jesus purchased with His life blood. The enemy has been defeated and you and I, who did not give our lives become "MORE THAN CONQUERORS!" But as we savor the victory, we are reminded of the final words of the valiant warrior; "Occupy till I come." Jesus did not leave us in the land of defeat; He left us upon the field of victory that He conquered through His death. Our responsibility is to hold that secured land until He comes again; which He will do!

We want to make our last day a good one so let's begin, as usual in prayer asking God to unveil the flesh of our eyes and open up our heart to receive truth today. Seek His blessings upon your study and pour out yourself in His Word. You have trekked with me for eight weeks of study and I applaud you, my sweet friend…I applaud you loudly! When you have finished your time in the prayer chamber we'll delve into His Word of study.

One last time together, let's hold up our left hand and make our declaration of the five unseen resistances. Write these out as final sealing of truth upon your heart.

Left Hand of Resistances

1._____

2._____

3._____

4._____

5._____

How does it help you to know your five unseen resistances? How should you use these five truths in Spiritual Warfare?

_____

_____

_____

Now lift up the right hand of power and authority and declare the five defensive weapons, your precious armor of God! Write these out after you have made your proclamation.

1._____

2._____

3._____

4._____

5._____

Clasp your one and only offensive weapon with your right hand of power and declare it aloud for what it is! Confess the truth of prayer that puts in motion every weapon given to you by the Lord. You are a mighty woman of war, beloved...a mighty woman of victory secured eternally by Jesus Christ upon the battlefield of your bondage. Declare His victory in your life and to the enemy when he approaches to launch an assault. Today, I want us to thread together all that the Lord has been so gracious to show us in our weeks of study. Look up the following verses and note what truth you learn from each. Take time to rest and meditate upon each one and how it fits into Spiritual Warfare and all that we have learned. Note how they relate to warfare!

Matthew 28:18

_____

_____

Colossian 1:27

_____

_____

John 15:5

_____

_____

I John 4:17

_____

_____

John 16:11

_____

_____

II Corinthians 15:57

_____

_____

James 4:7

_____

_____

What confession of truth can you write out, based on all that we have just looked over…again! How do these all tie together for you as God's soldier?

_____

_____

_____

_____

Fully acknowledging your God-given state of rulership, fully armed and fully surrendered to God, you will not be defeated by the enemy, no matter how intensive the war becomes. The victory is not ours to secure, it is ours to defend. Fill in the blanks with your name and read this declaration out loud.

I _____ am a child of God.

I _____ have overcome those who are in the world

Because greater is He that is in _____ **than he**

that is in the world.

We must understand what kind of woman we were created to be. In the Garden of Eden, God allowed everything for food but one kind of tree; the knowledge of good and evil. What was God saying by this command? Truth is not up for discussion! This tree held good knowledge and bad knowledge (evil). Truth is an anchor and God never puts it into the hands of His creation to devour and do with as they please. Truth is guarded and must be revered at all cost. Knowing the truth that He has allowed us to partake of through the study of His Word, we must acknowledge it is not ours to change, alter or manipulate for personal gain. We are women of war and we have all that is necessary to occupy and stand firm. This is unalterable truth, beloved! This brings us to our principle for today.

*P*RINCIPLE

I AM A WOMAN IN A WAR ALREADY WON

You are an heir of God, precious one. You are a joint heir with Christ. Begin to claim that privileged position of victory. Satan is absolutely powerless. He has no ability to do anything in your life except what he deceives you in and what you voluntarily yield to. Satan is waging a war that he has already lost. As we draw near to the end of this age, the spiritual forces of wickedness and world forces of darkness and all heads of evil are attacking with a vengeance because they know their days of freedom are numbered. But, no weapon formed against us will prosper!

What position has God placed you in? What were we created to do?

_____

_____

_____

Were you created to be ruled over by anyone but the Lord, Himself?

_____

_____

What has God done for you to ensure your success in occupying until He comes?

_____

_____

_____

Until we arm ourselves with truth, we will continue to live defeated in the war Jesus won for us long ago. Declare victory upon your battlefields and watch the enemy flee. Turn to the following verses and note what you learn from each. I must give you fair warning, these are slapping verses!

Deuteronomy 33:27

_____

_____

Psalm 71:18

_____

_____

Jeremiah 17:5 & 7

_____

_____

Isaiah 62:8

_____

_____

Luke 1:49-51

_____

_____

PRINCIPLE: I AM A WOMAN IN A WAR ALREADY WON

LIFE APPLICATION

I AM TO STAND IN HIS TRUTH

Where you stand will determine your victory over the enemy. Stand on ground that has been won by the blood of the Lamb and the victory is there for the taking. Stand upon the ground of the earthly and you will wage a war that you will never win. What's beneath your feet, beloved? Take a good look and take note where you have planted your feet, O Woman of War! Declare the praises of truth and watch the enemy flee before you, as you stand steadfastly in the principles of God's Word.